THE ALBION
Miscellany

THE ALBION
Miscellany

*Baggies Trivia,
History, Facts & Stats*

DAVE BOWLER & LAURIE RAMPLING

THE ALBION
Miscellany

All statistics, facts and figures are correct as of 5th May 2010

© Dave Bowler and Laurie Rampling

Dave Bowler and Laurie Rampling have asserted their rights in accordance with
the Copyright, Designs and Patents Act 1988 to be identified as the authors of this work.

Published By:
Pitch Publishing (Brighton) Ltd
A2 Yeoman Gate
Yeoman Way
Durrington
BN13 3QZ

Email: info@pitchpublishing.co.uk
Web: www.pitchpublishing.co.uk

First published 2010

A catalogue record for this book is available from the British Library.

10-digit ISBN: 1-9054116-7-7
13-digit ISBN: 978-1-9054116-7-2

Printed and bound in India by Replika Press Pvt. Ltd.

Dedications

Dave: To Mom, Dad and Lisa for their love and support.
And to the great Ray Barlow and His Holiness, Tony Brown.

Laurie: To my wife Marian, for her patience once again. For my boys Mark, Darren
and Stuart, always an inspiration; and Mum and Dad, for their early support.

FOREWORD BY BRENDON BATSON

I've been fortunate enough to have been involved with West Bromwich Albion for over 30 years now, since I joined as a player from Cambridge United in 1978. I was at The Hawthorns during a particularly exciting and important time, not just for the Albion, but for football as a whole and, as a result, it was a very special period in my life and career.

Even though it's more than 25 years since I last played, Albion has remained my club over the years and that bond remains as strong as ever through my involvement with the Former Players' Association.

Whenever we get together at games, at dinners, golf days or any other occasion, it doesn't take long before the stories start to flow amongst everyone and it's very easy to be transported back to the dressing room, the training ground or a particular game.

Some of those stories – they're not all fit to print! – are in the following pages, along with plenty of facts, figures and information about the club from its formation right through to today.

I hope you enjoy reading it, and that it will help answer a few quiz questions and brings back some good memories about a great football club and its rich history.

Brendon Batson, MBE

ACKNOWLEDGEMENTS

We would like to acknowledge the outstanding help and contribution of Albion sages Steve Carr, John Homer, Robert Bradley and in particular, that magnificent Albion historian Colin Mackenzie, who has spent countless hours in conversation going over many of the facts included in this book. His knowledge of all things Albion is supreme, and invaluable in the preparation of this book. Thank you gentlemen.

INTRODUCTION

What do you put in a 'Miscellany'? And, as one author has asked on several occasions, how do you pronounce it?

The answer to the first question was harder than the second. Do people wants facts and figures, do they want the offbeat, do they want stories about the great, the good and the Fernando Derveld? Should we relive great games, delve into the history books, or talk about the men around us now?

In the end, it's all of the above and a bit more. Like an Albion stew, marinating in some Albion herbs, served up on Albion china, washed down with a cup of Albion tea, this is the proverbial petit-dejener pour le chien. As Dana so very nearly had it when she won Eurovision; "All kinds of Albion remind me of you."

And that's what we have, bits of Albion history, of myth, of legend, of lists and records, of the legendary names and those who have barely scratched the surface of the Throstle nation, all there to remind you. Bite-sized morsels rub up against some longer tales. But comrades in the struggle to establish the People's Republic of West Bromwich at the summit of the Premier League, let this be your little blue book, let it inspire you in the months and years to come. Our struggle is just, and these are the philosophies upon which we build it.

So there you are. What's that? How do you pronounce it, you say? Me-sell-any. Will we? Too early to tell. Far too early to tell.

Dave Bowler & Laurie Rampling

IN THE BEGINNING

Over the years much speculation has been voiced about the formation of West Bromwich Albion Football Club, so much so that there has been much debate over whether the club began life in 1878 or 1879. It now seems an historic fact that Albion's very first game, as West Bromwich Strollers, was against Hudsons on or around November 30th 1878. Played locally, probably at Dartmouth Park, the game ended goalless. The Strollers team that day was given as: R. Roberts, G. Bell, J. Stanton, J. Forrester, H. Evans, T. Waterfield, J. Siddons, J. Stokes, S. Evans, E. Evans, W. Jones and S. Jones. There were twelve names on the team sheet, because as with most games of this era, they were played as 12-a-side, with a productive six-man forward line. Incidentally, the opposition, Hudsons, was a soap factory, situated in West Bromwich High Street. The company famously contributed to Albion's 'Shilling Fund' in 1905, and therefore, along with many other local businesses, have a lasting place in the club's history. Without them, Albion would almost certainly have gone out of business.

Things began to take shape for the 1879/80 season, the first fixture coming on October 25th 1879 against West Bromwich White Hart, which was won 7-0. This was followed by a further fixture against the same opposition a fortnight later, also won by a resounding 13-0. Then came the fixture against Black Lake Victoria on November 15th, which was also won, 2-1. The following week, Albion played Bullocks Foundry, winning handsomely 5-0, and followed up on November 29th with a 3-0 win over St. Phillips. There are no details of scorers, attendances etc, and even venue information is sketchy. The details that are known were gleaned from a local publication, the *Midland Athlete*, which has proved to be very comprehensive with available details of all football action in the region. Unfortunately, there is no clear confirmation on where these early games were played. Probably Dartmouth Park, certainly with regard to the Albion home games. Albion's next fixture, against Black Lake Victoria on December 13th 1879, was listed as a home fixture, and definitely played at Dartmouth Park. Albion won the match 1-0, and the report in the *Athlete* is the first recorded for an Albion match. In fact, this is the game that many mistakenly believed to be Albion's very first contest. Further research has now proved otherwise. The following week, Bullocks Foundry were the opponents. The match was also played at Dartmouth

Park, but is listed as an Albion away fixture. The game was drawn 1-1, and provides written confirmation of the club's first recorded goalscorer, Billy Bisseker, who for much of the season was Albion's skipper.

Albion's next two fixtures, the last of 1879, were against Wednesbury Robin Hood, at home, and West Bromwich St. Mary Magdalene Recreation, away. These matches were played on December 26th and 27th, respectively, and Albion defeated Robin Hood 6-0, but lost the following day 2-1. Albion moved into 1880, with a fixture against Wednesbury Robin Hood, away, on January 10th. The match was played at Hall Green, and ended in a 1-0 defeat. On January 24th, Albion played a return fixture against St. Mary Magdalene Recreation, at Dartmouth Park, winning the match 1-0, with an early goal by John Stokes. The following week, Albion played again at Dartmouth Park, against St. Phillips, but the 3-1 victory is listed as an away fixture. The *Midland Athlete* reports that Albion were a goal behind at the break, but came strong in the second half, running out 3-1 winners. Historian Colin Mackenzie points out that notable names in the St. Phillips side, Walker, Bunn and Crowley, would soon feature for Albion. Albion's next two fixtures, first on February 7th, were against Smethwick Holy Trinity, away, which was drawn 0-0, and February 21st, also away, to West Bromwich Rovers, ending in a 2-1 defeat. Once again, unfortunately, very little is documented about either of these two fixtures. Not so with Albion's fixture the following week, a return match against Smethwick Holy Trinity on Albion's soil. The game resulted in a resounding 3-0 win. Perhaps more importantly, it documents the club's first goal, by Bob Roberts. Roberts, of course, was later to become the club's first iconic goalkeeping legend but he did play a lot of his early football as an outfielder. Roberts' opener was followed by a second by either Jim Stanton or John Stokes – it is unclear which player had the honour – but the third by Billy Bisseker wrapped up what the *Midland Athlete* described as a "good all-round game by Albion".

On March 6th Albion played Smethwick Excelsior away, and in what was described as a "well contested game", ran out 2-0 winners with goals from Harry Aston and James Hampton. This result was followed up by a 5-3 home victory over Hearts of Oak on March 27th. The following week, Albion played a return away fixture against Hearts of Oak when the home side got their revenge, running out 3-1 winners, with James

Hampton getting Albion's goal. The *Midland Athlete* also reported that Albion were deprived of the services of skipper Billy Bisseker but had found a good replacement in Whitehouse of West Bromwich Rovers. John Stokes deputised as captain. Moving into April, Albion entertained West Bromwich Rovers, on April 10th, for whom Whitehouse was now playing. The *Midland Athlete* reported that "Davies gave the visitors the lead shortly after half time, but just before the final whistle, Stanton made a splendid shot, and Evans headed it through the posts." Thus, the result was a 1-1 draw. On April 24th, Albion played their last match of that historic first campaign by entertaining Christ Church second team and ran out 3-1 winners, with, unfortunately, only the Christ Church scorer, Treadwell, being named in the *Midland Athlete* report.

ONE HIT WONDERS

Most Albion supporters would give anything just to play one game for the club they follow, but as a professional, sights need to be set rather higher than that. Unfortunately, some have only played that single game for the Throstles in the league or the cup. Excluding any current players, trialists, or those who joined on loan, these are the one hit wonders: Sam Allardyce (as a sub), Gilbert Alsop, Norman Aldridge, Vitle Andersen (as sub), Arthur Appleby, George Askin, William Arch, Geoff Barnsley, Bill Bowser, Jack Boyd, John Burns, Edward Burton, George Bushell, Christopher Charsley, Ben Clark, George Corbett, Fred Crabtree (scored on debut), Arthur Crump, Arthur Davenport, Rob Davies (as sub), John Dawes, Harold Dicken, William Folks, Ernest Ford, John Foster, Graham Easter (as sub), Sam Edwards, Sam Farrington (scored on debut), Harold Guy, Michael Gallagher, Darren Goodall (as sub), Sean Hayward, Ernest Hoyland, Abraham Law, Michael Lee, Tony Lowery, Joseph Mathews, James Millar, Harry Oliver, John Parry, James Thomas Pemberton, Richard Pike, James Pittaway, Gilbert Price, Alexander Ramsey, John Rea, Paul Reece, Arthur Richards, Robert Hugh Roberts, Eric Robinson, Michael Rodosthenous (as sub), John Screen, Bartosz Slusarski (as sub), Stan Steele, Archie Styles, John Swallow, Charles Shaw (scored on debut), Arthur Sheldon, Marc Sinfield, John Smith, Griffith Taylor, John Tighe, Arthur Trevis, Isaiah Turner, Samuel Turner, Gavin Ward, James Whitehouse, George Willetts, Norman Williams, Billy Williams, Harry Wood (scored on debut).

A SPECIAL TALENT

Jonathan Greening was a well loved and respected member of the Albion side over many years, skippering the club to the Football League Championship title in 2008. But aside from his ability on the field, Jono had a special talent for enlivening press conferences with his surrealist turn of mind that posed many a philosophical conundrum that had the journalists guessing. One of his more intriguing statements came on the subject of music. "How can people still write new songs," he asked. "Surely they've used up all the notes by now?" On a pre-season trip to Portugal, he quite sensibly asked; "Have they got a different sun here to the one we've got at home? This one's much hotter." Also a wiz with the SatNav, on agreeing to pick up Kevin Phillips on his way into training one day, he wondered why he'd been driving for an hour and was heading north on the M6. Phoning Phillips, who only lived round the corner from Jono, he asked if he was going the right way, only to realise he'd entered Uttoxeter rather than Uttoxeter Road into the machine.

THE GENERATION GAME

Only two sets of father and son have played together in the same game for the Throstles. The first pairing was 1954 FA Cup winner George Lee and his son, Michael, in the Central League game against Bury at The Hawthorns on August 28th 1957, Albion falling to a 2-0 defeat despite the presence of other FA Cup winners Jimmy Dudley and Jim Sanders. Three years later in September 1960, the same pairing featured for the third team in a Warwickshire Combination game against Netherton. The Baggies won 5-0, all the goals coming from Woodburn who never managed to get promotion even as far as the Albion reserve team, never mind the first XI. The second example of a multigenerational Albion outfit came on March 17th 1992 when Albion played a friendly against the Gibraltar FA XI at the Victoria Stadium in Gibraltar. Albion won 4-0 thanks to goals from Bob Taylor, Graham Harbey and a brace from Neil Cartwright, while in the second half, goalkeeper Jonathan Gould was joined on the pitch by his dad, the then manager Bobby. Nobody knows what the Barbary Macaques on the rock made of it all.

KEEP YOUNG AND BEAUTIFUL

The Baggies have made much of their reputation as a cup-fighting team over the years, and that extends to the FA Youth Cup where Albion have made it all the way to the final on three occasions. Albion's first appearance in the final came in the 1954/55 season, but their timing was off if they thought they could carry off the trophy. They ran straight into Manchester United, a group that was to win fame and meet with tragedy as the Busby Babes, the jewel in the crown being Duncan Edwards, born and brought up in nearby Dudley. The Throstles were well beaten in the first leg at Old Trafford on April 27th 1955, losing 4-1, the consolation coming from an own goal by Wilf McGuinness who was later to manage the Red Devils. Albion's team was: Cashmore; Whale, Rogers; Drury, Hughes, Cooke; Maynes, Setters, McCartney, Jackson and Graham Williams, playing on the wing before his later conversion to full-back. For the return game at The Hawthorns three days later, Setters moved to right-half in place of Drury and Harris took over at inside-right. Unfortunately, United proved to be far too strong and won 3-0 giving an overall aggregate win of 7-1. Of the side put out by Albion over the two legs, Maurice Setters (later to join United), Chuck Drury, Alec Jackson and Graham Williams went on to play regular first-team football for the club and Williams skippered the side to the League Cup and FA Cup in the space of two years from 1966 to 1968, as well as captaining Wales. Jackson represented the Football League, and Setters was capped at under-23 level for England.

In 1968/69, as the senior team missed out on a second successive FA Cup Final by falling at the semi-final hurdle, the club's youngsters made their mark by reaching their final where they faced Sunderland. The first leg at The Hawthorns on April 28th 1969 ended with the fledgling Throstles earning a 3-0 lead, Hughie McLean and Stewart Woolgar, with two, getting on the scoresheet. Albion's team that day was: Gordon Nisbet in goal (before being converted to full-back); Minton, Bell; Hughes, Holton, Robertson; Woolgar, Hartford, Morton, Cantello, McLean. Butler was substitute. In the second leg, the wheels came off of Albion's challenge when the Rokerites demolished the Baggies 6-0. The team remained the same, if the score did not. Only Bell, Morton, Holton and Butler failed to make the grade through to the first team, although Jim

Holton later joined Manchester United. Minton, Woolgar and McLean had only limited opportunity and success in the first team but Nisbet, Robertson, Hartford and Cantello went on to amass an astonishing 1,437 appearances between them. Nisbet represented England at junior level, Len Cantello won England under-23 honours, and Hartford played for his native Scotland. Neither Bell nor Morton played league football.

Albion's last appearance in the final came in the 1975/76 season as their senior brethren won promotion back to the First Division. The two-legged final against Wolverhampton Wanderers was never really a contest. In the first leg at Molineux on April 27th 1976, Albion coasted home 2-0 thanks to goals from Summerfield and Tranter. Albion's team was: Grew; Cooper, Statham; Loveridge, Clarke, Davies; Lynex (Hood), Gregson, Tranter, Hughes and Summerfield. The second leg was played at The Hawthorns on May 3rd 1976. Albion made one change, Derek Monaghan coming into the side for Lynex, who was injured in the first leg. Monaghan was later replaced by Hood. The result was a comprehensive 3-0 victory, making the overall aggregate a very satisfying 5-0 as Albion lifted the trophy. Although Cooper played in one first-team friendly, he never played league football, and nor did Clarke and Tranter. Loveridge, Gregson and Hood never featured in the Albion first XI, but played league football elsewhere. Mark Grew, Derek Statham, Steve Lynex, Wayne Hughes and Derek Monaghan all made it through to the first team, but only Derek Statham became an established first choice with 378 first XI appearances to his name, and ten goals. He also obtained England honours at all levels whilst at Albion; Wayne Hughes was also capped at under-21 level by Wales.

THE MAINE EVENT

Other than the original Wembley Stadium, the long-departed Maine Road ground, former home of Manchester City, is the only neutral ground where Albion have played both FA Cup and League Cup ties. In 1968, the Throstles played their victorious second replay against Liverpool in Manchester, winning 2-1 and qualifying for the semi-final thumping of Birmingham City. Ten years on, Albion returned to Maine Road for a League Cup second-round second replay against Leeds United. This time the forces of good were defeated by a single goal.

ABSOLUTELY FABIAN

In the case of Fabian De Freitas, Andy Warhol was wrong. De Freitas had two 15 minutes' worth of Albion fame, one at either end of the sliding scale; glorious and catastrophic. On second thoughts, perhaps each burst of celebrity lasted seven-and-a-half minutes and Warhol got it right – he was a pretty shrewd cookie after all. It all started so well too, even though when Albion boss Denis Smith was toying with the idea of bringing De Freitas to The Hawthorns way back in August 1998, all we knew of him was his brief spell at Bolton Wanderers where he had been a colleague of fellow Dutchman, Richard Sneekes. Given that Richard had already become something of a legend amongst the Albion faithful, there was some optimism that lightning would strike twice. Here initially on loan, De Freitas made his debut at Port Vale, coming on for the last three minutes after a Lee Hughes hat-trick had won another game in Staffordshire. The following Saturday Fabian took his place on the bench for a game against Norwich City. Things were locked at 0-0 after 59 minutes when Smith decided it was time to have a longer look at just what De Freitas could do for us and introduced him to the fray in place of the goalscoring machine that was Mickey Evans. Thirty seconds later, De Freitas had pounced on a rebound after a Hughes header hit the bar and had put Albion into the lead. And if that wasn't enough, just 13 minutes later our new hero had got on the end of a James Quinn knock down and drilled in his second goal of the afternoon and effectively sealed the three points. For those final 18 glorious minutes, The Hawthorns rang out in tones of exultation, safe in the knowledge that we had found a new messiah who would surely take us unto the Promised Land. Two chants alternated: "Sign him up, sign him up, sign him up!" was the first, but then we really got over excited. "Are you Cyrille in disguise?" Er, as it turned out, no, not exactly…

Albion signed him up from Spanish club Osasuna and sat back and waited for the goals to pour in. And waited. And waited. But we had to learn the virtue of patience for only five followed over the rest of the season, two of those coming in the final two games of the campaign. But by then, Fab had already enjoyed the remaining seven-and-a-half minutes of glorious, immortal celebrity. Perhaps it was fitting that a man who came here as a saviour should hear the death knell over Easter. Well, not quite the death knell perhaps, but quite clearly he didn't hear the phone. The Throstles were at home on Easter Monday, welcoming Crewe Alexandra for a fixture that was all but meaningless even though there were still seven games left to play in the season – that's how we did it back then, none of this last day, seat of your pants excitement that Albion go in for nowadays. Being a midweek game, De Freitas believed it was a 7.45pm kick-off. Being a Bank Holiday Monday, the rest of the world believed it was a 3pm kick off and, on this occasion, the majority view prevailed. While Fabian slept soundly in his bed, dreaming no doubt of what he was going to do to the Crewe defence that evening, Albion officials were glued to the phone, trying to find out where our centre forward was. Legend has it that given it was a Bank Holiday, we even sent a search party to the Ikea, but this cannot be confirmed at this time. Not wishing to wake him as he was so deep in his preparations for the game, his girlfriend either a) ignored the phone, b) turned the ringer off or c) spent all afternoon talking to a friend so that nobody could get through, depending on which story you prefer to believe. In fairness, we can think of a few other Albion players where we would have been thrilled if they'd overslept every week, but that's another story. As a result, the Throstles fielded Lee Hughes and Mark Angel up front, all of our carefully thought-out plans thrown into disarray. I can't imagine how it happened, but we lost 5-1 that afternoon. Spectators rushed onto the field, doing themselves and the game no good, but finding time to throw a shirt at Smith in the dugout and a few season tickets onto the turf. After the game, there were protests in Halfords Lane, the likes of which hadn't been seen since WMPTE changed the timetable for the 79. Thereafter, Fabian was never late for kick-off again... Until Gary Megson arrived at the Albion as the new manager after the brief Brian Little interlude and advised him that there was no point in him getting out of bed again.

HIGHS AND LOWS

Albion have played the great and the good of English football's league clubs over the last 130 years or more. But what are the best and worst wins and defeats in competitive games against each club?

Accrington Stanley	5-1	7/3/1891	0-3	25/1/1890
Arsenal	7-0	14/10/1922	2-6	18/9/1970
Aston Villa	7-0	19/10/1936	1-7	24/4/1899

Barnsley	7-0	11/11/1989	0-3	13/4/1906
				6/5/2007	
Birmingham City	7-1	18/4/1960	2-7	20/2/1905
Blackburn Rovers	8-1	18/1/1936	2-6	22/9/1888
Blackpool	7-1	28/4/1962	1-5	3/3/1956
Bolton Wanderers	7-2	8/12/1900	0-7	7/12/1889
Bournemouth	4-0	1/11/1991	1-2	22/2/1992
Bradford City	6-1	11/11/1905	0-5	19/12/1914
Bradford Park Avenue	7-1	16/4/1949	1-5	4/1/1930
Brentford	4-0	12/8/2003	0-3	19/8/1998
Brighton & Hove Albion	5-0	1/9/1982	1-3	10/3/1993
Bristol City	4-1	21/11/2009	1-3	10/2/1906
Bristol Rovers	5-1	9/3/2008	1-2	22/10/1974
Burnley	8-1	11/11/1967	1-6	8/9/1951
Burton United	6-0	21/4/1905	0-2	27/4/1907
Burton Wanderers	23-0	1/2/1890	undefeated	
Bury	6-0	11/3/1939	3-7	11/9/1926
Cardiff City	6-1	21/11/1953	2-4	10/11/1923
Carlisle United	3-0	3/4/1976	2-3	25/1/1975
Charlton Athletic	4-0	1/9/1930	1-5	11/2/1955
Chelsea	5-2	17/4/1929	1-7	3/12/1960
				24/10/1953	
Cheltenham Town	1-0	16/2/2002	undefeated	
Chester City	3-1	10/4/199	undefeated	
Chesterfield	5-2	24/11/1906	1-3	18/2/1939
Colchester United	4-0	31/1/1968	1-3	3/9/1996
Coventry City	7-1	21/10/1978	2-4	23/9/1967
				27/8/1968	
Crewe Alexandra	4-1	26/3/2002	1-5	5/4/1999
Crystal Palace	3-1	20/9/1969	0-4	10/2/1973
Darlington	3-1	22/12/1991	undefeated	
Darwen	12-0	4/4/1892	1-2	11/11/1893
Derby County	6-0	11/12/1886	3-9	8/12/1934
Doncaster Rovers	6-1	24/9/1904	1-3	3/4/1948
Everton	6-1	7/12/1935	1-7	30/12/1893
Exeter City	6-3	17/8/1992	1-3	31/10/1973
Fulham	6-1	24/11/1946	1-6	11/2/2006
				8/9/1962	

Gainsborough Trinity ....7-0.......5/10/1901 .... 2-4 ..... 1/10/1904
Gateshead ....3-0.....17/12/1927 ....undefeated
Gillingham..........................3-1.....18/11/2000 .... 1-2 ... 29/12/2001
Glossop ....6-0.....24/2/1906 .... 2-3 ... 26/4/1910
Grimsby Town ....7-0.........2/1/1909 .... 1-5 ... 31/8/1998
Halifax Town ....5-1.....24/8/1999 .... 1-2 ... 14/11/1993
Hartlepool United...............3-1.......3/11/1992 .... 1-3 ... 26/8/2008
Hereford United ....unbeaten .... 0-1 .... 7/9/1994
Huddersfield Town ....5-1.......23/4/1938 .... 1-5 ... 23/10/1920
Hull City............................7-1.......19/4/1930 .... 1-5 ... 23/4/1910
Ipswich Town......................6-1.........9/3/1963 .... 0-7 ... 6/11/1976
Leeds United.......................6-3.......6/10/1934 .... 0-5 ..... 18/2/1967
Leicester City......................6-0.......13/3/1965 .... 2-6 .... 6/5/1933
Leyton Orient ....5-0.......6/10/1906 .... 1-3 .... 3/3/1992
Lincoln City........................5-0.........8/9/1948 .... 1-3 .... 7/1/1961
Liverpool ....6-1.......1/2/1936 .... 0-6 ..... 26/4/2003
Luton Town ....4-0.......23/2/1957 .... 1-5 ... 14/12/1957
....24/10/1959 ....
Manchester City ....9-2.......21/9/1957 .... 1-7 ..... 16/4/1938
Manchester United ....6-3.......29/4/1968 .... 0-7 .... 8/4/1970
Middlesbrough....................5-0.......19/9/2009 .... 0-4 ..... 16/3/1974
Millwall..............................6-1.....26/12/1929 .... 1-4 ..... 6/10/1990
Newcastle United................7-3.......16/9/1953 .... 1-5 ... 21/11/1931
.... 14/9/1938
.... 26/11/1949
Newport County.................7-2.......28/9/1946 ....undefeated
Northampton Town.............4-2.......23/8/1995 ....undefeated
Norwich City......................5-1.....18/12/1996 .... 1-4 ... 21/11/1995
Nottingham Forest..............8-0.......16/4/1900 .... 1-6 ... 20/10/1900
.... 7/10/1989
Notts County ....8-0.....25/10/1919 .... 1-8 ... 19/11/1892
Oldham Athletic..................3-0.......21/3/1921 .... 0-5 .... 1/1/1930
Oxford United ....3-0.......28/9/1974 .... 0-3 ..... 29/9/1998
Peterborough United ....4-0.......17/9/1991 .... 0-3 ... 31/8/1988
Plymouth Argyle ....5-1.........5/1/1963 .... 1-5 ..... 31/1/1931
Portsmouth ....6-2.......17/9/1958 .... 1-6 ... 14/12/1954
Port Vale.............................4-1.......28/4/1906 .... 1-8 .... 9/3/1929
....6/4/1931 ....

Preston North End ....4-0.........2/1/1960 .... 0-5 ... 26/12/1888
.... 5/10/1889
.... 26/2/1895
Queens Park Rangers...........5-1.....30/9/2007 .... 1-3 ... 6/3/2010
Reading ....5-0.....30/3/1909 .... 3-5 ... 17/11/1928
Rotherham United..............4-0.....30/1/1954 .... 1-2 ... 17/11/2001
....31/8/1977 ....
Scunthorpe United..............5-0.....29/12/2007 ....undefeated
Sheffield United ....7-1.....26/1/1935 .... 0-6 ... 19/2/2000
Sheffield Wednesday...........6-0.....22/4/1895 .... 0-6 .... 2/1/1893
Shrewsbury Town ....4-0.........2/1/1989 .... 1-2 ..... 20/4/1987
....22/10/1991 ....
Southampton ....5-1.........3/5/1930 .... 0-4 ... 26/8/1967
.... 17/2/1977
Southend United.................3-0.....11/12/1993 .... 1-3 .... 1/1/2007
Spennymoor United............7-1.....16/1/1937 ....undefeated
Stockport County ....5-0.....16/2/1935 .... 1-5 ... 20/2/1993
Stoke City ....6-0.....18/12/1988 .... 3-10 ..... 4/2/1937
Sunderland.........................6-4.....27/2/1937 .... 1-8 ... 22/10/1892
Swansea City.......................6-2.....26/10/1929 .... 1-6 .... 2/2/1929
Swindon Town.....................3-1.........3/9/1988 .... 2-5 ..... 19/3/1995
Torquay United....................2-1.........9/2/1993 ....undefeated
Tottenham Hotspur.............5-0.....12/2/1927 .... 0-5 ..... 17/3/1951
.... 18/4/1959
.... 28/10/1970
Tranmere Rovers.................5-1.....30/4/1995 .... 0-3 ..... 2/11/1993
.... 6/11/1999
Walsall...............................6-1.........1/2/1900 .... 1-4 ..... 9/8/2003
Watford.............................5-0.....31/10/2009 .... 1-5 ..... 24/8/1985
West Ham United..............7-1.....24/10/1925 .... 1-6 ..... 16/4/1965
Wigan Athletic ....5-1.....24/4/1993 .... 1-3 ... 2/10/2002
Wimbledon........................3-1.....24/10/2000 .... 1-4 .... 9/1/1988
Wolverhampton Wanderers 8-0.....27/12/1893 .... 0-7 ..... 16/3/1963
Wrexham...unbeaten .... 0-1 ..... 11/1/1930
Wycombe Wanderers..........4-3.....21/9/1999 ....undefeated
York City............................3-1.....12/4/1975 .... 2-3 ..... 22/1/1938

COME ON YOU BAGGIES

At the beginning of the 1910/11 season, many Albion players were released as the club looked to build a new, promotion-challenging squad. One of those upon whom the axe fell was long-serving full-back Amos Adams. Amos had given the club sterling service since signing from Springfields in 1897, making a total of 214 first-team appearances, scoring three goals and becoming a fine defensive partner for his international skipper Jesse Pennington. Amos retired from the English game and later had some success in coaching and management with Amiens SC in France, before resuming his connections with Albion as a scout, and then working on the groundstaff. However, he had an even greater claim to Albion fame, for it would appear that he was unwittingly the instigator of the club's other nickname, the Baggies, according to long-serving club secretary Ephraim Smith, whose explanation of the origin of the nickname was printed in the Throstle Club News, a booklet published by the Albion supporters' club, back in 1968.

Smith wrote; "In 1904, when the Albion were known as the 'Throstles', they had a stocky back by the name of Amos Adams. His thickness of hips made his 'baggy' pants look even more huge and one day when he was not playing well, a fan shouted 'Baggy!' Albion and Adams recovered quickly, but the name stuck. Albion officials and players hate the nickname. We like being called Albion or the Throstles, and we hope fans will cease using this term of 'Baggies'." Smith's appeal for a return to the proper nickname failed, though many long-serving supporters will sympathise given the Throstles nickname is certainly the embodiment of the club and its move from Stoney Lane, to the throstle-inhabited patch of ground at the corner of the Birmingham Road and Halfords Lane which we all now call home, and which is presided over by the throstle perched on the ball in the Woodman Corner of the Birmingham Road End.

There are two other variations of the Baggies theme, however. One is that 'Baggies' is a corruption of Magee, namely Tommy, the former Albion stalwart from the 1920s and 1930s. Another is that the name stems from the time the Albion supporters toured local public houses collecting funds from supporters in little bags when the club was faced with extinction in the early 1900s. The cry "Here come the baggies" is said to have been heard ringing out around the pubs.

THE FRAGRANT MR GLIDDEN

Tommy Glidden was an FA Cup and promotion-winning captain as a player and later saw the Throstles bring the cup home in his capacity as a club director, chalking up an association of more than 50 years with the club, service now recognised in the Glidden Suite in the West Stand, named in his honour and filled with images of his time as a player at The Hawthorns. But beyond that, he has further distinction as perhaps the only Albion man to have a flower named in his honour, although quite why it is that the horticulturists have ignored the claims of such delicate flowers as John Kaye or Sean Gregan, it is hard to imagine. At the 67th annual Birmingham Chrysanthemum Show, held in 1932, three new variations of the flower were exhibited, and all of the new varieties were named after local footballers – Birmingham City's Joe Bradford, Aston Villa's Billy Walker and Albion's skipper, Tommy Glidden – clearly the best of the bunch. The bloom dedicated to Tommy was described as a "large white flower", and named simply "The T. Glidden". Surely now is the time for Monty Don to inspire a revival.

YOU AGAIN!

It's not uncommon to meet a team three or maybe four times a season if the cup draw pairs you up with a side from your division, but Albion have become even more intimately acquainted with some teams over the years. Three times, we've met a club on five occasions in the one campaign. In 1930/31, Albion doubled over Charlton Athletic in the league, and drew twice with them in the FA Cup, before winning in a second replay. In 1974/75, there were five meetings with Norwich City, winning 5-1 in the Texaco Cup, losing 2-0 in extra time in a League Cup replay, and drawing at The Hawthorns and losing at Carrow Road in the league. Then in 2006/07, Albion played five games against Wolves, winning four – one league, two play-offs and one FA Cup – and losing once in the league. When it didn't really count. In 1952/53, Albion played six games against Chelsea, two in the league – one win each – and then three FA Cup draws before the Blues won the third replay in what is Albion's longest-ever FA Cup tie. The record for a single season is seven meetings which happened in 1978/79, a season when Albion couldn't get away from Leeds United. There were three League Cup ties before Albion were beaten, two FA

Cup ties before Albion won through in extra time – both played at The Hawthorns as Leeds were banned from playing FA Cup games at home – and twice in the league; one win each. We got pretty familiar with the Hammers over two seasons though. In 1965/66 and 1966/67, Albion played West Ham a total of eight times, four league games of course, plus the two-legged League Cup final of 1966 and the two-legged League Cup semi the following year, Albion triumphing in both ties.

THE EARLY BATH

Sendings off have become increasingly prevalent as the authorities continue to take steps to take much of the physical contact out of the sport. In addition, referees tend to apply the laws of the game more stringently than in the past under the glare of the television spotlight. Whatever the reason, dismissals are being dished out far more regularly so it's no surprise to find that the king of the red card is a player of recent vintage – Paul Robinson. Robbo was sent off on six occasions for the Throstles, the first in a League Cup tie in October 2005. Some 368 days later he was on his way to the dressing room a little ahead of schedule after a controversial red card at St. Andrew's, but it was only four months before he was collecting another one, in a home game with Sunderland – that decision was later reversed. Paul had a busy Christmas and New Year in 2007/08, being sent off against Coventry at The Hawthorns on December 4th 2007 and then getting the marching orders at Hull City on January 12th 2008. Red Robbo's final red card came against Manchester United at The Hawthorns in January 2009, a ludicrous decision that was swiftly rescinded. Given that was the second time that happened to him, his red card count might be considered to be just the four, but that would still see him heading the disciplinary list along with Willie Johnston and Daryl Burgess. Johnston left Rangers for the Albion after his career in Scotland saw him sent off perpetually in front of the SFA. Looking for a new start, Willie toned down his act a little bit but he was still perfectly capable of getting himself into trouble. His first dismissal came against Swindon Town in September 1973 and four months later, he was off again, this time in an FA Cup replay against Everton. He was sent off at home to Bristol City in November 1974 but it was almost two years until his fourth and final dismissal which came in a grand manner. Frustrated as Albion were becoming victims of a

League Cup giant-killing at home to Brighton & Hove Albion, Willie tried to kick one of the officials in the backside, missed, then walked off without even waiting for the inevitable. God love him. Burgess was more a victim of changing times, a big defender for whom sendings off were the same kind of occupational hazard as arrest was for Norman Stanley Fletcher. Daryl had to do porridge on four occasions too, firstly after a red card against Bolton Wanderers in November 1993. He was sent off at the City Ground against Nottingham Forest in October 1997, then took the long, lonely walk twice inside three months in the autumn of 1999 after being red carded at home to Wycombe Wanderers in the League Cup and then at Norwich City in the First Division. Four Albion men have managed a hat-trick of dismissals; Len Cantello, Carlton Palmer, Darren Bradley and Neil Clement.

EUROPEAN SPECIAL

Undeniably, one of the most admirable changes that the Premier League has ushered in is the ability of our clubs to attract some of the finest footballers from all over the globe rather than watching a constant stream of our best players heading off abroad as we had to during the 1980s. Only 25 years ago, the chances of seeing the very best the world could offer came around but rarely. There was no saturation coverage of European football, while the world's best either stayed at home or migrated to Italy or Spain. Your only hope of seeing the best in the flesh was if your club qualified for Europe, had a decent run, and drew the sides you wanted to see. Unless you supported Liverpool, or maybe Forest under the immortal Brian Clough, then those runs didn't happen all that often. In truth, Albion have probably only enjoyed one great European Cup run, for though we competed strongly in the Cup Winners' Cup in 1968/69, they were ties where we didn't really meet the cream, going out to Dunfermline in the last eight. Our greatest European days came in 1978/79 – without a shadow of a doubt – and perhaps our finest moment came in a game which Brendon Batson still proclaims his most memorable 90 minutes in an Albion shirt. "I suppose that from that era, everybody thinks about the Manchester United game at Christmas in 1978 when we won 5-3 up at Old Trafford. But overall, I think the most memorable game that I played for Albion was just before that one, when we went to play out in Spain against Valencia in the Uefa Cup. From start to finish, from the time the draw was made, from the time we travelled out there to the time we came back, everything about it was right. We were up against a Valencia team that included Mario Kempes who, a few months earlier, had played the central role in winning the World Cup for Argentina – he was absolutely in his prime. They had Rainer Bonhof in the team too, a brilliant West German midfielder, as well as some excellent Spanish players, and they really were one of the most glamorous and exciting teams in Europe at the time, as well as being one of the very best.

"Albion hadn't been in Europe for a long time and so we didn't have an enormous amount of experience in the squad as far as that went. Tony Brown had played at that level, Willie Johnston had actually scored in a European final when he was at Rangers, but after the problems he had at the World Cup in Argentina in 1978, he was banned from playing in European competitions. So it was all very new to the vast majority of us. For me in particular it was a big step up. I'd only come to the Albion that January after playing in the old Third Division with Cambridge United. We qualified for Europe after the 1977/78 season was finished in fact, because if Liverpool hadn't beaten Bruges in the European Cup final, we wouldn't have been in the competition at all! But that season, I was still trying to get myself into the team and it was only really with the start of 1978/79 that I became a first choice, so it was a very exciting time. I'd been playing at the lower end of English league football and then suddenly, I was getting ready to take on some of the best players in the world and that was just terrific for me and for all of us."

The prospect of welcoming Kempes to West Bromwich was a startling one, enough to persuade some hardy kids to stand in Halfords Lane on the Tuesday night before the game in order to get autographs after they'd finished training under The Hawthorns' lights the night before the second-leg game. By the time that second leg came around, we were starting to think that an astonishing win might actually be possible. Yet the mood of Albion supporters when the draw was made had been much less optimistic.

"When the draw came out, I think the feeling among the supporters was that, it's a great draw, we'll get to see Mario Kempes and then we'll get beaten and we can worry about the league and the FA Cup after that. But funnily enough, among the players, we really did believe we could come

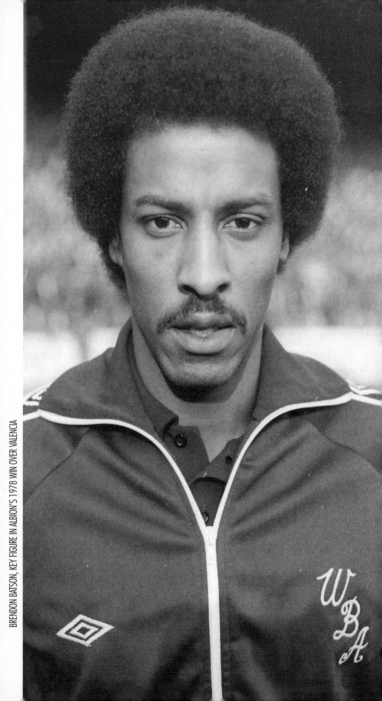

through. At that time, we were playing some wonderful football, we were full of confidence both as individuals and as a team, and we genuinely weren't frightened of anybody. Everybody was very excited, but none of us thought they would be too good for us. On top of that, we were very pleased that we were playing the first leg in Spain and that we could then bring them back to The Hawthorns. We were well prepared, Big Ron used to get us well briefed about the opposition, we had them watched, but we were most concerned about playing our own game. We wanted to do our work, not worry so much about them. There were no special plans made for Kempes before the game, because we never really did that, whoever we were playing. We knew what he was capable of and we were aware of his strengths, but we didn't go out to man-mark him out of the game or anything like that. He had a habit of dropping off and floating back into the midfield, and the general feeling we had was that wherever he was, up front or in the middle, we had to pressure the ball. That was something we did as a team anyway, we liked to win the ball as high up the pitch as possible. Tony Brown will admit he was no Roy Keane when it comes to tackling, but Big Ron would just tell him to stay on his feet, make himself a nuisance to their defenders, so we didn't let them relieve the pressure on themselves, we harried them even after they'd won the ball from us and one of our attacks had apparently broken down. The thing that we were most aware of was Bonhof and his ability at free kicks because he had a shot like thunder, so we did what we could not to concede needless, cheap free kicks around the box.

"I remember Ron doing his team talk before the game, talking about us doing it the way Liverpool always approached away games in Europe, keeping it tight for 20 minutes, silencing the crowd, and we'd just started doing that and I think they got their goal just about halfway through the first half, just as we were starting to think we'd done some of the hard work. I don't think I'd ever seen oranges on the pitch before, but when they scored, the crowd started hurling oranges right away in celebration! We were defending the goal in front of their noisiest supporters and when they did score, it was deafening, it really was. Saying that, I don't recall there being any racism out there at the time, I didn't come off the pitch thinking 'God, I wouldn't want to come back here again.'"

Valencia's goal came 15 minutes into the first period, Kempes instrumental, his corner being headed in by fellow Argentinean, Felman. A setback for sure, but Albion were good enough to gather themselves together, ready to get back into the game.

"I remember thinking about what Ron had said about keeping them quiet, but he'd also said that if they did score, we just had to regroup, not drop our heads and just carry on playing the way we always did, to keep looking to get a goal of our own if we could. That took the pressure off us and we just kept on playing our game and gradually got back into it. I think you have to say that it was a terrific Albion performance all through the team – that was the basis. But then that night, I think Laurie Cunningham gave one of the greatest displays of football that I've ever seen from a single individual, he was absolutely frightening that evening and, as events turned out, that was the night he sold himself to Real Madrid. That game changed Laurie's life and it's such a pity that it wasn't captured on film. Only those of us who were there that night will know how good Laurie was, but take it from me, he was incredible. Down the right side, there was Laurie, Lenny Cantello and myself and I remember looking at Laurie and thanking God that it wasn't my job to mark him that night because he was sensational. It had all the ingredients, a night match, under lights, terrific atmosphere and it just seemed it was his stage. Every time we got the ball out to him, we knew he had the beating of everybody in their team; they didn't know what to do with him. In the context of the game, the opposition, the job we had to do, I can't think that I've ever seen anything better.

"Even after they'd got into the lead, I never felt that they were running riot at any stage and I think right through the side, we all realised that Laurie was in such good form that night that if we could just keep getting the ball over to him as much as possible, there was a way back into the game for us. He could hold the ball for long periods once he had it and that gave us a breather, gave us a chance to re-organise ourselves and then to launch fresh attacks. Laurie was outstanding but there were loads of great performances right through the side, back to front, and ultimately it was that team display that was crucial. You can't win big games if you don't play as a team, you have to play for the cause rather than yourself. It was right that Laurie got our equaliser, right at the start of the second half, because he was in such incredible form, and I remember that as we came off the field, I felt very confident that we could come back to The Hawthorns and finish off the job. We were very buoyant in the dressing room, we felt that away goal had given us enough to see them off in the second leg, because we knew they had to come out and score if they were going to win. We knew an away goal was important and once we had that, coming off the pitch we thought we'd done well. Overall, I thought it was a game where we played really well, probably at our very best, both in terms of keeping control of a very good side, and in imposing ourselves on them when we could. Their goal aside, I honestly don't remember us having too many scares to deal with at the back because we kept the game under our control."

Having got back on terms, if any side was going to win, it was Albion, but ultimately, the 1-1 draw we brought back to England represented an impressive night's work, a night completed by an enjoyable trip home.

"We flew out on Aer Lingus, and I think in recognition of our achievement in the game, on the way back, all the duty free actually was free, and that capped the whole night because we enjoyed a little celebration on our way home!"

There were celebrations in every right-thinking household in the Midlands a fortnight later as Albion trounced Valencia 2-0 in the return courtesy of Tony Brown. Albion fans began to allow themselves dreams of a Uefa Cup win. But it all went horribly wrong against the rather less gifted, but infinitely more worldly-wise, Red Star Belgrade…

PEERLESS PENNINGTON

It's hard to come up with a definitive Albion legend after so many great players have represented the Throstles over the last 130 years and more, but if you were forced to create an identikit picture of the archetypal Baggie, it would probably look something like Jesse Pennington. Nicknamed 'Peerless' because of his stylish, cultured play, Jesse had a nineteen-year career at the Hawthorns, in which he amassed a fantastic 455 appearances, a club record which stood for many years until Tony Brown came along. Had it not been for the Great War, which cut his playing career by four years or more, he would surely have amassed even more for his beloved Albion. Jesse never scored a goal in first-class

football for Albion, although did miss his one opportunity, a penalty away at Leicester Fosse in December 1904. Pennington also appeared in 39 FA Cup ties, one FA Charity Shield match, 12 war-time fixtures and approximately 30 other matches. A wonderful club man, he picked up an FA Cup losers' medal in 1911/12, and then, of course, held the league championship trophy aloft in May 1919 after a tremendous 4-0 victory over Chelsea. Albion actually clinched the title after a 3-1 win over Bradford City at the Hawthorns some weeks earlier.

Born in West Bromwich in 1883, he first signed as an amateur for Aston Villa in 1902. He signed for Albion as a professional in March 1903, and made his debut in September the same year. Jesse won 25 England caps between 1907 and 1920 and skippered his country on two occasions. During the Great War, he turned out as a 'guest' player for Oldbury Town, and helped organise many charity matches, one such coming in Wednesbury, at Easter 1916, in aid of the victims of the Zeppelin raids at Tipton. His wonderful career came to an end in May 1922, when his doctor diagnosed an enlarged heart and a duodenal ulcer and advised him to give up playing. So at the grand old age of 39, Jesse turned his attention to coaching for the 1922/23 campaign. Whilst engaged in his coaching duties he recommended that the youthful Tommy Glidden should be switched from inside-left to the right wing. Another amazing piece of foresight was to recommend a promising young centre forward playing at Hartlepool United to the Albion board – W. G. Richardson. In the 1930s Jesse concentrated on his Stourport poultry smallholding, but in 1938 he returned to what he knew best, and at 55 took an FA coaching refresher course with many of his old playing contemporaries, maintaining his links with the game he had served for so long. In August 1963, he was presented with a cheque by Albion directors on the occasion of his 80th birthday and received a gift from the Sports Writers' Association, and appeared on local television to talk about the occasion and his life in football. In 1964 his life story was serialised in the *Sports Argus* and in April 1965 he was guest of honour and pulled the first pint at the opening of the first 'Throstle Club'. Three years later, on May 18th 1968, Jesse was a guest of the club at the victorious Wembley victory over Everton. Sadly that was the last time he was seen by his Albion public, passing away on September 5th 1970, in Kidderminster Hospital, after a long illness.

BRING ME SUNSHINE

Few will question that by 1992, the Throstles were in the doldrums and that the inspired appointment of Osvaldo Ardiles by the then chairman, Trevor Summers, was the perfect antidote to years of decline, years where the smile was systematically wiped off the face of the football club. We'd endured relegation from the top flight, the arrival of Ron Saunders and the decimation of the playing squad, the Woking debacle, Bobby Gould, the Twerton Park catastrophe, dull, dour, aimless football and all played out at The Hawthorns which had hitherto been a temple dedicated to an expansive, exciting game. Ardiles lifted spirits on the terraces and in the dressing room, as Bernie McNally, one of his key players, remembers. "He was wonderful in training, everyone came in smiling, even if you weren't in the side. I was in charge of the kitty so every now and again Ossie would say; 'Bernie, get £50 from the kitty and tomorrow at training, we have egg and bacon sandwiches.' There was a great camaraderie among the players and we still have that bond about us now whenever we get together.

"It was about playing with a smile – pass, receive, move – playing proper football but above all else, enjoying it. I had a spell just before Christmas when I wasn't playing particularly well, and you get a bit down about it. He called me into the office after training, so I sat down and he said, 'Bernie, you are a very smiley person, but at the moment, you are not smiling enough. This reflects in your football. If you do not smile tomorrow, I fine you £50.' So the next day, I had to make sure I was smiling, and I must admit, it was great psychology and it worked for me – my form started to pick up. He had that knack of going to different people and saying things to get a reaction from them, and that worked for him most of the time. I think that was the fundamental change to a team that hadn't been going anywhere the previous year, because there weren't too many changes in personnel really. Ian Hamilton, Steve Lilwall, Kevin Donovan came in – Andy Hunt right at the end of the season – but he transformed the players that were already here by giving us the freedom, the belief and the responsibility. That was the first time anybody had told me I was a good player, that I could get on the ball, pass it around, link up, and that was a huge boost for me, it was very encouraging.

"He insisted that we play the game his way. We'd have a five-a-side on a Monday morning and I can remember once or twice getting the ball when I was on the goal-line, the legs start wobbling, and I remember knocking it long, 50 metres to the front guys, just to clear it. Ossie would start shouting 'Wimbledon! Wimbledon!' When we got in the dressing room, he'd say, 'Boys, what do you think? I think we should sell Bernie to Wimbledon because he was rubbish this morning, just smashing it forward!' All the lads would take the mickey, but it was a great atmosphere. We all knew he was a great player in his time. From seeing him at Tottenham, he'd won the World Cup with Argentina and obviously, he was on a different level to us. But he was so composed, had so much time and he tried to instil that in us for match situations, even in the heat of a game. If you were in your own box, he'd say; 'We do not panic, we do not slash at the ball. We get the ball down, very controlled and we slot the ball into Row Z, seat 73.' Because of that, you didn't snatch at things, you just put the ball into touch when you had no other options, all nice and calm.

"It was a great balance with Ossie and his assistant, Keith Burkinshaw, the dour Yorkshireman. They worked fantastically well together. Ossie would give his team talk before we went out, and it was all, 'Bernie you go forward'. While he was saying that, Keith would be behind him, looking at you, shaking his head and mouthing at you, 'No you don't!'

"Keith would give us his talk before Ossie, and he'd go on a bit, all about the shape, who you were picking up, playing offsides, all that kind of thing. One day, he'd been going for five minutes, and Ossie started looking at his watch. Another couple of minutes, Ossie started yawning. Ten minutes, and Keith finally stopped. Ossie took over and said, 'Everything that Keith says, it's rubbish. We go out, we play, we score goals! Play!' And Keith would just roll his eyes! Keith's English mentality and Ossie's drive to get forward just made a great mixture for us. It was a shame it didn't last longer."

GOLDEN GLOBE

Winning the FA Cup has been celebrated in many ways down the years, but way back in 1892, Albion were pretty out there when it came to milking the very most out of flattening Aston Villa in the FA Cup Final

to the tune of three goals – count 'em – to a big, fat nil. In the immediate aftermath of it all, the club grabbed hold of a tin of gold leaf that they'd kept on file for just such an occasion, covered the match ball in it – and then had a suitable inscription painted upon it so that nobody was left in any doubt that those Villa boys had take one hell of a beating. Still, there was something missing. And so, the club summoned up a throstle, allowed it a hearty breakfast and a final ciggie, and released the contents of a Magnum 45, the most powerful handgun in the world, upon it. Sadly, there wasn't much of the throstle left after that, so we fetched another one, poisoned its trill, waited for it to fall off the perch and join the choir invisible, stuffed it and glued it on top of the ball. How's that for post-modern Mr Damien Hirst? All of which leaves one question unanswered. Never mind winning the FA Cup, where's our Turner prize got to?

THE SATURDAY MEN

Once upon a time, football was played in black and white. It's true. Even the blues were a lighter shade of black, the grass was either a vibrant shade of black if it was August, or a flat muddy black kind of colour if it was January. Supporters wore hats at all times, be they men or women, and very often hurled them into the air when goals were scored, leading to them returning home wearing an altogether different style of bonnet to the one they'd left the house in, causing some husbands to have to do some substantial explaining work to a wife waiting by the cooker wielding a rolling pin. Goalscorers were greeted by strong, manly handshakes and a pat on the back, missed chances saw hundreds of supporters instinctively cover their eyes so shocked were they, and there were no tedious phone-in shows, merely collections of old men in local cafes discussing tactics, false teeth clacking as they did so, others sucking on gums long since untroubled by enamel. Children, this is not a time wherein dinosaurs roamed the earth, but a vision of the game as it was played less than 50 years ago, back in the early 1960s, back before The Beatles arrived and invented colour. Fortunately, it's also an era that was caught on film, by the Ford Motor Company of all things, the motor manufacturer funding a series of documentary films that looked to capture various slices of British life back in early 1962, from shop floor to football field.

"The Saturday Men" was one of them, a very early example of the fly on the wall school of film making, *cinema verite* of a kind, where the cameras went behind the scenes and simply rolled. The club who opened their doors to the film makers was us, West Bromwich Albion, an established top-flight club with England internationals such as Bobby Robson, Don Howe and Derek Kevan in their midst, FA Cup winners just eight years before. The film captured them on the training pitch, in the dressing room afterwards, before and during matchday, as well as going in and around the Black Country to see what the supporters made of it all and just what the players did away from the game. As a document of its time, it's fascinating. The voiceover talks of professional football being an occupation where its members value status and cars above all other things. Not strictly true: at the time, the maximum wage had only just been abolished and club captain Robson, about to set off to the 1962 World Cup, used to walk to work from the club house he lived in. He was on the princely sum of around £25 a week. Nonetheless, film of star midfielder Alec Jackson back home in Tipton captured a sense of dislocation between a working-class lad who'd made good and the friends and relatives he'd left behind playing snooker in the local club. Although Alec continued to go there for a frame or two in an evening, "he's no longer liked as much because of his success" we are reliably informed. Thankfully, having met and talked to Alec in those very same Tipton environs in recent times, I can inform you that the voiceover was 100% wrong, because few men are better liked than Jacko.

Elsewhere, there's Stuart Williams, coming towards the end of a distinguished career that clocked up more than 30 caps for Wales. With an eye on the future, after training, he heads off to sell machine parts for a local company, "trading on his name because local buyers all want to talk to a footballer". At the other end of the age scale is youngster Clive Clark who spends his afternoon roaming the streets with nothing to do, "waiting nervously for Saturday". Watching Clark, it's easy to see where Richard Lester might have got his ideas from for the 'This Boy' sequence of *A Hard Day's Night*, the sequence that established Ringo Starr as the actor amongst the Fab Four. Other highlights include Don Howe on his life as a stripper; "You get up in the morning and get dressed, come to work and take your clothes off and get changed. Work, take your clothes off, get changed go home. Take them off again to go to bed in the afternoon. Get up, put them on, have your tea…" A busy life in the Howe household clearly. Then there are the locals, discussing tactics in the cafe owned by former Albion cup-winning striker Teddy Sandford. "Playing him theer? It's like tekin' the sugar out of a mon's tay while he ay lookin'!" A bygone era, a simpler era. For better or worse, it's long since gone, but the atmosphere seeps through every second of this half-hour film, a little gem now captured on dvd.

POLE TO POLE

The youngest player ever to represent Albion in a first-team fixture – albeit a friendly – is Lateef Elford-Alliyu who played against Stafford Rangers aged 15 years and 61 days on August 1st 2007. He also scored on his debut. The same fixture also saw James Hurst (15 years, 182 days) and Romaine Sawyers (15 years, 271 days) make their debuts for the Throstles too. In a competitive game, Frank Hodgetts was 16 years, 26 days old when he scored on his debut in a wartime regional game with Notts County on October 26th 1940, Albion winning 3-1. But in a 'proper' senior game, the record for the youngest Baggies goes to Charles 'Tug' Wilson who was 16 years and 73 days old when he made his full league debut in a First Division game at Oldham Athletic on October 1st 1921. Sid Bowser became Albion's youngest-ever FA Cup combatant at 16 years 359 days old when he faced Bolton Wanderers on January 16th 1909, Albion winning 3-1. Mickey Lewis was 16 years, 303 days old when he became the youngest Throstle in a League Cup tie at Crystal Palace on December 15th 1981. Spookily, Albion won that one 3-1 too. At the other end of the spectrum, Ronnie Allen was 66 years, 115 days old when, on May 10th 1995, he played in the Pied Piper appeal friendly against Cheltenham Town, coming on as a substitute. In a competitive game, George Baddeley was 39 years, 345 days old when he played in a 1-1 draw in a First Division game against Sheffield Wednesday on April 18th 1914, the oldest Albion player in a competitive game, a record that Dean Kiely will break should he feature for the Baggies in a game after September 20th during the 2010/11 season. Kiely was 39 years, 191 days old when he came on as second-half sub for Scott Carson on April 17th 2010 against Middlesbrough, his most recent game to the end of the 2009/10 campaign. 'Peerless' Jesse Pennington was 38 years and 183 days old when he became the oldest player to represent the Baggies in the FA Cup when he played against Notts County on February 22nd 1922. Nigel Spink was 39 years, 19 days old when he achieved a similar distinction by playing against Cambridge United in the League Cup on August 27th 1997. Spink was also the oldest Albion player on his debut at 37 years, 179 days when he played against Ipswich Town on February 3rd 1996.

FEEL THE BENEFIT

Down through the years, players have benefited from testimonial matches, the proceeds of which were designed to aid them financially once their playing days were over. Players of the past did not have access to the money that is in the game today, so these were much needed funds. Plenty of Throstles have been aided by benefit and testimonial games orve the years, a reward for years of loyalty and long service.

Date	Player	Opponent	Score	Attendance
25/4/1892	Tom Pearson	Birmingham & District XI	2-2	3,500
3/3/1890	George Timmins	Birmingham & District XI	4-1	4,000
17/10/1892	George Woodhall	Birmingham & District XI	2-1	3,500
27/11/1893	Billy Bassett	Sheffield Wednesday	2-1	4,852
26/11/1894	Sam Nicholls	Blackburn Rovers	3-1	1,400
18/11/1895	Roddy McLeod	Aston Villa	1-1	3,000
7/4/1896	Jack Horton	Stoke City	3-1	2,000
18/10/1897	Joe Reader	Aston Villa	2-0	3,000
14/2/1898	Billy Williams	Wolverhampton Wanderers	1-1	4,000
31/10/1898	Tom Perry	Aston Villa	2-0	6,237
29/10/1900	Billy Richards	Wolverhampton Wanderers	3-3	5,000
30/11/1901	Jack Paddock	Small Heath	2-0	2,047
3/3/1902	Ben Garfield	Select XI	4-2	1,000
20/10/1902	Harry Hadley	Aston Villa	1-5	8,674
26/10/1903	Charlie Simmons	Aston Villa	3-3	5,000
25/12/1903	George Cave	Select XI	1-1	4,500
20/10/1906	Arthur Randall	Stockport County	1-1	12,300
24/10/1908	Jesse Pennington	Leeds City	2-1	13,554
11/11/1911	Freddie Buck	Woolwich Arsenal	1-1	13,900
22/3/1912	Hubert Pearson	Bradford City	1-1	6,565
20/12/1913	George Baddeley	Bolton Wanderers	1-1	15,311
28/3/1913	Jesse Pennington	Sunderland	2-1	23,366
4/5/1921	Bill Barber	Wolverhampton Wanderers	2-0	3,106

1/11/1954	Jack Sankey	Hereford United	5-10 ..4,500
25/4/1956	Norman Heath	International XI	5-5...55,497
28/4/1965	Graham Williams	WBA XI	4-6...10,160
15/5/1967	Bobby Cram	All Stars XI	6-5.....3,943
6/5/1974	Tony Brown	Wolves/Birmingham XI	2-1...11,901
8/5/1975	Ray Wilson	Aston Villa	2-2.....9,133
29/10/1975	Jeff Astle	Albion 1968	1-2...11,941
8/5/1978	John Osborne	John Giles XI	0-2...12,302
15/5/1979	Len Cantello	Cyrille Regis XI	2-3.....7,023
29/4/1980	Ally Robertson	Wolverhampton Wanderers	3-1.....5,110
4/5/1981	John Wile	Select XI	2-3.....6,961
30/4/1984	Brendon Batson	Aston Villa	1-2.....4,600
5/5/1986	Tony Godden	WBA 1978 XI	1-1.....2,158
7/10/1992	Martyn Bennett	Birmingham City	0-1.....2,842
9/5/1994	Gary Robson	Aston Villa	1-2.....7,321
6/5/1996	Stuart Naylor	Coventry City	3-2.....5,013
3/8/1997	Ronnie Allen	Aston Villa	1-2...16,864
23/5/1999	Tony Brown	Jamaica XI	0-1...20,358
27/7/1999	Paul Raven	Sheffield Wednesday	1-2.....2,489
8/5/2001	Darryl Burgess	Newcastle United	0-3.....4,440
13/5/2003	Bob Taylor	Bryan Robson All Stars	7-2...16,017

BORE DRAW

Since Albion began competing in the Football League Cup in 1965/66, they've played the same team in both cups in the same season on four occasions. In 1966/67, it was Northampton Town. Albion won both games 3-1, both at Northampton, in the League Cup quarter-final and the FA Cup third round. In 1978/79, it took Leeds United three games to dispose of Albion in the second round of the League Cup, but the Baggies got revenge by beating Leeds in a fourth round FA Cup replay. Derby County knocked Albion out of both cups in 2001/02, winning on aggregate in the second round of the League Cup then winning 3-2 at Pride Park in round three of the FA Cup. The Throstles knocked Peterborough United out of the two competitions in 2007/08, winning 2-0 in the League Cup and 3-0 in the FA Cup, both at London Road. Albion then beat them in the FA Cup the following season for good measure.

TO BE FRANK

As a kid, is there any bigger dream than scoring the winning goal in the FA Cup Final at a packed Wembley Stadium? Actually making it happen is a million-to-one shot. Frank Griffin turned that dream into reality when he strode forward and placed that shot in a million into the Preston North End net on May 1st, 1954 bringing the trophy back to the Midlands and ensuring that the 'Team of the Century' did not end that celestial campaign empty handed. With three minutes to go in that final showpiece fixture of the season, Albion and Preston North End were locked at 2-2, injury time looking all but certain. Yet in almost every game, a late chance comes calling. On this day it called for Griffin, as he recalled; "I was resigned to extra time. Suddenly, Joe Kennedy sent a pass to Reg Ryan who chipped the ball forward to me. I cut in without really knowing whether I would shoot or centre. As I passed full-back Joe Walton and got into stride, I saw an opening. Immediately I slammed in a scoring shot – and turned to see my colleagues tearing towards me with beaming smiles. Arms wrapped round me, I was nearly strangled, and gasped for breath as the lads pummelled and smacked my back. I had won the cup in the last seconds. Could there be a greater moment in a player's life?"

That goal was precious relief for an Albion side who had long led the First Division throughout the 1953/54 season, only to disintegrate as injuries and international call-ups took a heavy toll on the team. The side that had been chasing the double – they would have been the first to achieve it in the 20th century – eventually had to settle for second place and there were fears as the Baggies headed for Wembley that a season of majestic football would end without a prize. Griffin's goal dispelled that nightmare scenario, putting the icing on a magical day for him, a day when Albion's outside-right outshone his Preston counterpart, England's Tom Finney, the man who, along with Stanley Matthews, denied Griffin the England cap his talents deserved.

Griffin was an old-school winger back in the days when teams played with two men hugging the touchline, looking to beat the full-back for pace or trickery, then arrow in crosses for one of the three inside-forwards to get on the end of. Albion were a little bit out of the ordinary in that regard – Ronnie Allen anything but the conventional battering ram centre forward – but the precision of Griffin's crossing was still a potent weapon, allowing Allen and Johnnie Nicholls in particular to dart into the box and crash shots past many a helpless goalkeeper. That was the signature of a majestic side, all pace, intelligence, sleight of hand, integrity of purpose. And Griffin was at the heart of it.

Frank Griffin, born on March 28th 1928, joined the Throstles from Shrewsbury Town in April 1951, only a month after he first turned professional, having previously played for Eccles Town. He was plucked from that comparative obscurity by manager Jack Smith as Albion looked desperately for a replacement for another great right-winger, Billy Elliott, at the end of a career savaged by war. Griffin made his debut for the club in the final game of the 1950/51 season, a 1-1 draw at Roker Park, but by the time the following season came around he was very much a fixture in a team that was beginning to mature, heeding the call to greatness: Allen, Nicholls, Ryan, Lee, the great Ray Barlow, Millard and Rickaby were all present and correct alongside Griffin. Frank was steady as Albion made a faltering start to the campaign, winning only twice in the first 12 games. But then the number seven stepped up to the plate with six goals in five games as Albion beat Portsmouth 5-0, won 5-2 at Anfield and beat Manchester City 3-2 to slowly climb the table.

Griffin took his fine goalscoring form into the next season when first Jesse Carver, and then Vic Buckingham, took charge as Albion embraced a Continental style reminiscent of the mighty Hungarians; Frank's pace, ease on the ball, and intelligent running making him a perfect fit. The Baggies finished fourth that season and were poised for an assault on the title itself. Frank played a big part as Albion pursued the double scoring seven goals, including one in the legendary 7-3 win at Newcastle, before scoring the most important one of all, the one that captured the FA Cup. The team evolved further in the years that followed, new faces such as Bobby Robson, Don Howe and Derek Kevan coming to the fore, but Griffin remained a regular contributor to the side, making and scoring goals until the competition that brought him his lasting fame showed a more capricious side of its nature, taking away his career. Against Sheffield United, in a fifth-round FA Cup replay on February 19th 1958, Frank suffered a broken leg in two places, an injury that rarely mended well in

those days when surgery was rather less sophisticated than today, far more intrusive, and rarely as successful. He played half a dozen more games in the stripes, collecting one last goal in a 4-2 win at Preston on January 31st 1959, but the burst of acceleration, that special bit of devilment, had gone out of his play forever and First Division full-backs now had the measure of him. It became increasingly clear that his time at The Hawthorns was coming to a close and that he would play out his career in the lower divisions…

In the summer of 1959, Griffin left the Throstles for Northampton Town for a final season in the lower leagues, before playing non-league football for Wellington Town. His Albion career amounted to 275 first-team games and 52 goals, but like so many of his era, his legacy goes far beyond mere figures. The flickering black and white film images that we still have of Griffin's devastating directness, his powerful shot and his eye for a chance, tie us to our heritage, offer a glimpse of one of the truly great Albion teams of all time. Frank Griffin's goal that won the 1954 FA Cup is one of the immovable, rocklike foundations upon which we continue to build this football club. That goal, and all that it meant, continues to provide us with our inspiration, offering us aspirations for a future when future Albion heroes emulate that feat. Griffin will be immortal for as long as the game of football matters in this country. He scored the winning goal in the greatest cup competition that there is. He won the FA Cup. He set the standards that every club must aspire to. Every football-mad lad in the country wants to grow up to be Frank Griffin, even if they've not yet heard of him. But they will. Because the names of FA Cup winners echo down the decades. We are all standing on the shoulders of giants. Giants like Frank Griffin will never leave us.

THE FLOWERS OF MANCHESTER

West Bromwich Albion and Manchester United somehow seem to be inextricably linked. When a big moment in one's history dawns, the other seems to have a part to play. George Best's debut, and then his valediction, came at Old Trafford with Albion in the supporting cast. Our Premiership bow was made against the Red Devils. We set off for our glorious Wembley days in May 1968 with a pulsating game between us at The Hawthorns a few weeks earlier still fresh in the memory, Albion triumphing 6-3. The glorious side of 1978/79 reached its zenith at Christmas by demolishing United 5-3 on their own turf. And Albion were also at United's side in March 1958, just a few weeks after the tragedy on the airfields of Munich had turned a Manchester United side from likely conquerors of Europe to a team with – literally in too many cases – no future, in the blink of an eye. For the Throstles and United were pitted against one another three times in seven days. In the wake of such catastrophe, football seems such a trivial little pastime, and yet it was the game that gave those left behind a reason to go on, offering a momentum to their ultimate and necessary recovery, providing purpose. As the front cover of the *United Review* proclaimed on March 5th, "United will go on". After all, what other choice is there for a great institution?

That plane went down in Munich on February 6th, a disaster that sent shockwaves far beyond the environs of Manchester, right across the country and into the heart of the footballing community, wherever they played the game. Graham Williams was a young player starting to make his way into the Albion team, while simultaneously doing his duty elsewhere, as he recalls. "I was doing my National Service and Bobby Charlton was in the same camp with me, Duncan Edwards as well. In 1955, Albion had played United in the FA Youth Cup final, so we had history with them and I had a lot of feeling for those boys. I vividly remember hearing the news – I can't remember where I was when Kennedy was shot but I remember when I heard about United's plane. We'd just finished a regimental game, we were coming in to eat afterwards and somebody said the United plane had gone down. The shock was horrendous, everybody trying to find out who had survived. We lost friends, not just footballers. It was very early in the days when people started flying to games. People were frightened of flying anyhow, so when that happened, it sent a shiver through everybody. A few years earlier, Torino had lost a team in another crash, so purely from that point of view, as a footballer, you were a bit worried about your team going abroad and having to get on a plane yourself."

United had a side that was loved at that time, even by the neutral, an age long before much of the populace became jaundiced by their Premiership success. The recipe for that far reaching admiration? Youth, excitement and genius as Graham Williams explains: "Manchester United were such a side at that time. They played great football, they were very exciting, and they were all very young men with their best football still in front of them. The Busby Babes were going to be the biggest thing we'd ever seen in England because they were a beautiful footballing side, had great skill, and were lovely to watch. Early in the 1950s, it had been Albion who had nearly done the double in 1954, Wolves were a big side as well, but United were overtaking us both, so they would have become huge anyway.

"Eddie Colman could send a whole stand out of the ground with the way he swerved, a brilliant player. Tommy Taylor was some centre forward. They were playing here one time when I was still just a youngster and I watched them training, preparing, and to see what he could do was just incredible. Van Basten was about the closest I've sent to Tommy, that's how good he was. He had a brilliant scoring record for United and England and he would have gone on to do amazing things in the game. Then there was Duncan. Duncan Edwards was from just down the road, from Dudley, and it's a pity he didn't come here instead of going to United! He was such a great player. You have to be careful because the tragedy, the fact that he died so young, the fact that he played so little football, it all turns him into a legend and we shouldn't. We should remember him for the great player he already was because that's more than enough. He was a man, not a cartoon. Duncan gets bigger every year, the more we talk about him, but he actually was a giant, he really was. He played against us in that youth game in 1955 and he murdered us because he was already a man. We were in awe of him even then. We had a great youngster called Barry Hughes that people were expecting great things from, but Duncan destroyed him and the rest of us. He was in the England side at 18, I remember going to see him play for England at Wolverhampton, he was just so mature and he wasn't out of his teens. Here was a player that could have played in the World Cup in 1966, maybe in 1970 as well. A truly great player."

All those possibilities were laid to waste in the German ice and fog, but football waits for nobody. With the team decimated – and manager Matt Busby lying in hospital and unlikely to recover – United was being run by another Albion connection, stalwart of the 1930s, Jimmy Murphy. A new United had to take up the baton and play out the fixture list. Given their plight, league football became almost an irrelevance, for it was obvious that they would be unable to capture the consistency necessary to challenge for a third straight title. But the FA Cup was something else entirely. In the first post-Munich fixture, United somehow overcame Sheffield Wednesday winning 3-0 to put them into the sixth round. Nobody wanted to come up against them. We did, as Graham Williams remembers...

"Getting drawn against United meant you were on a hiding to nothing because everybody in the country wanted them to go and win the FA Cup after Munich. They were suddenly the underdogs, everybody felt for them and everybody wanted to see them get to Wembley. It was a big task for them because they had to assemble a new team, though they were given special dispensation to loan and sign players from other clubs, but obviously they couldn't bring in anyone of the quality of the players they'd lost. Jimmy Murphy took over while Matt Busby was recovering and he changed the style of play to reflect that. They became very physical and, without being unfair, I think they'd admit that for the rest of the season they could get away with a lot because of the sympathy vote, and I don't think anybody begrudged them that – unless you were on the other side!"

At least the Throstles had home advantage as a crowd of 58,250 crammed into The Hawthorns on March 1st, 1958. Those that were there were privileged indeed, for this was a pulsating tie of the kind that made the FA Cup's reputation. One reporter, caught up in the hysteria that surrounded United, said it was second only to the 'Matthews Cup Final' of 1953, adding; "This was not the football of ordinary mortals. This was the stuff of wonder men... the nectar of the gods." The game started as it meant to carry on. Ernie Taylor, one of Murphy's buys, gave United a sixth-minute lead that was snuffed out by Ronnie Allen six minutes later. United's rag bag of first, second and third teamers, mixed with a batch of new signings, gave Albion as good as they got – no mean feat given that this was a magnificent Albion side, cup winners themselves just four years earlier. The peerless half-back line of Jimmy Dudley, Joe Kennedy and the great Ray Barlow, the genius of Ronnie Allen, augmented by England internationals Don Howe, Bobby Robson and the Tank, Derek Kevan; a side of all the talents.

But destiny's call is a powerful thing and United's players realised they were playing for something bigger than a mere victory. They were playing for the future of a football club, an energising force that gave them the drive and the energy necessary to snatch the lead just before the break, Taylor beating Jim Sanders with a thunderous drive that smacked off the bar and to the feet of Dawson for a tap-in. The Throstles took up the chase in the second half, goalkeeper Harry Gregg – who had helped colleagues to safety out of that Munich plane – taking on the altogether safer task of keeping Albion at bay with a string of fine saves until, in the dying minutes, he couldn't hold a shot, left-winger Roy Horobin darting in to pick up the pieces and secure a replay, though controversy raged over whether the ball crossed the line – later photographs proved it had. And then what a replay, a game etched in the minds of those who went through it, including Sir Bobby Robson who recalled the game instantly, nearly 50 years on. "The club, the city was in distress, it was sad to see. People flocked to Manchester to support the new Manchester United and what was left of it, the survivors. Hysteria abounded in the city, that was the only word for it, hysteria."

Graham Williams adds; "Going to Old Trafford was the last thing we needed with all the emotion that surrounded it. It was a Wednesday night game and the gates were closed at 4.30 in the afternoon! There were 20,000 outside the ground, locked out without a ticket. The place was heaving. We were coming in on the team bus as usual on the day of the game. We drove up to Knutsford, had the pre-match meal and then we had a police escort from there. But we couldn't get anywhere near the ground, it was that thick with people around Old Trafford. We were an hour late getting in because of that and the match had to kick off late." The facts of the game are that United shaded the first half, but as time wore on Albion took control, Ronnie Allen causing mayhem by roaming across the pitch, twice denied by brilliant saves from Gregg, then creating the best chance for Derek Kevan, Gregg throwing himself at the feet of the Tank to snatch the ball as he prepared to shoot. With time almost up, Bobby Charlton, having switched to the right flank, slung in a low cross, finding Colin Webster unmarked to tap in. The game barely had time to restart. United were through.

Reflecting on the night half a century on, Sir Bobby believes; "There was no way we could win that match. No way West Bromwich Albion, that night, could win the match against Manchester United, at Manchester. It was like taking on the world."

ONE OF THE GREATEST ALBION CAPTAINS, GRAHAM WILLIAMS

Graham Williams has similar memories: "There was a big sympathy vote for them. We played really well, outplayed them, did pretty much everything right except score. It was 0-0 going into the last minute and then Bobby Charlton broke away down the right and squared the ball for Colin Webster who scored when he was standing a mile offside, but no referee on earth would have disallowed that one!" Maybe United's bravery earned that victory. Certainly in Harry Gregg, Bill Foulkes and Bobby Charlton, men who got off the plane and back onto the field, they had characters made of granite, great men that football should never, ever forget, as Williams agrees: "I think for the likes of Bobby, Bill and Harry, it was a relief to get onto the football field and just play, to just put all that other stuff out of their minds for 90 minutes and get back to doing what it is that you do. You can sit around and mope, but I think it was a big relief for them to play again. Bobby was frightened of flying for a long time afterwards and he didn't talk about the whole incident for many years. Bill still finds it very hard. When we were up there in November for the tribute to George Best, Wilf McGuinness brought the subject up and he was saying that some of those involved still can't talk about it without getting too upset. Harry Gregg was a different kind of character and I think it helped him to talk about what had gone on.

"Going anywhere with footballers is an experience, especially on a plane. Everybody is taking the mickey, the banter is going on, everyone is joking. But they tried to take off three times and by the third time, I imagine it must have been sombre anyway. Those that didn't fancy flying anyway would have been forced to get on the plane for the third attempt and then that happens. That must be a hard thing to come to terms with, especially when you've survived when your friends haven't. But if anything positive came out of Munich, it was that United became something more than just a club, it became almost a mythological thing, people wanted to be part of the rebirth. They could attract players very easily – Maurice Setters went from here the following summer. Maurice fitted in perfectly because United became a physically harder team for a couple of seasons until the next generation came through a few years later, with the likes of George Best. From there on, United have always wanted to bring their own players through because it follows in the footsteps of the Busby Babes, it's a tradition of sorts, as is the demand to play exciting football. The side United have now is terrific, they have some great players. I know that as you look back, the players of your time get better, but to me, the only current player I'd put in the Babes' team would be Ryan Giggs. He's a Welshman after all!"

The following Saturday, there was a league game to play at Old Trafford, making it three games in seven days. Sir Bobby Robson: "Let me tell you a story. Three days later, we went back to Manchester United in an ordinary league game, with the same team and beat them 4-0. I haven't looked that up, it's off the top of my head and I can remember that occasion so well. On Wednesday, a hysterical night, a monumental evening for Man United, we couldn't win. Could not win. Three days later we walked it." The outpouring of emotion on the Wednesday did for United, Albion strolling to a win with two from Allen, one from Kevan and an own goal by Ian Greaves. Albion's affair with United wasn't over, for the club called on its followers to help those who had been lost in the tragedy. *Albion News* noted that; "It is the Albion supporter's turn next Saturday to show what he is made of. To pay his tribute to those so cruelly shattered in that Munich disaster. With the help and co-operation of the Supporters' Club, we will collect for the Manchester United Disaster Fund at the entrances on Saturday next, when we play Everton. Dare we hope that our supporters will do their best to reach the top of the table." The supporters responded superbly to the tune of £217, the Supporters' Club rounding it up to £250, which was sent to the Lord Mayor of Manchester, something of which we can be proud.

BURY MY HEART AT WOUNDED KNEE

On November 8th 1890, Albion travelled to Sunderland for an away league match. In goal for Albion that day was the great Josiah Reader. All through the game Reader was in scrapes with the opposition forwards and took plenty of stick from them before Hannah, the Sunderland forward, was chasing a through ball and Reader ran out towards the on-rushing forward and ball. As the 'Free Press' described; "It was clear that one of them must have it." In self-defence, Reader came out with his knee up and caught Hannah in the stomach, and the latter had to be removed from the ground to hospital by cab. The home spectators turned nasty and "they vented their feelings towards Reader, who had to be smuggled away from the ground". Reader was threatened after the game by a couple of hundred 'determined fellows' who were waiting outside, and so threatening was the abuse that the inspector of police said he would not be held responsible if Reader came out of the safety of the ground. Reader was eventually smuggled away in a cab secretly summoned by telephone, and reached the Queen's Hotel, in Fawcett Street, before the rest of the Albion side.

CARVE OUR NAME WITH PRIDE

Every self-respecting Albion fan knows the club started life as West Bromwich Strollers before taking on the name that now rings around the world, but over the intervening years, evil plans have been afoot to change it once more. Probably the best known effort came under the management of Don Howe in the 1970s when, following the reorganisation of local government and the introduction of Sandwell as the local council, it was suggested that we become Sandwell Albion. There are those who say that Albion's disastrous record of relegation, and then a flirtation with promotion, cost him his job in 1975 but frankly, that's piffle. It was this heinous desire to change the name of the club that forced us to show him the door. Yet more than 40 years earlier, amid the club's greatest season of 1930/31, the town itself was confronted by a sudden name change as a local weekly paper started to refer to the place as Westbromwich. While Councillor Crump, the mayor at the time, was outraged and said "this will never be countenanced officially", the local printers were unrepentant. "So far as we are concerned, we are a law unto ourselves, and we will continue to spell Westbromwich as one word in all our printing and stationery. We have long since dispensed with the full stop and comma in our letterpress, and other firms are following our lead! It is not a fad or an attempt to set a new fashion, it is simplified spelling, and saving of time and labour in the long run." The *Birmingham Gazette* poured scorn on the idea while hacking off the local citizenry by claiming that Bromwich meant "The abode of the broom". Local historians, the Carl Chinns of the day, queued up to complain pointing out that 'Bromwich', in fact, is the old name of Birmingham, hence 'Bromwycham', or now, Brummagem. He further pointed out that it was likely that the name refers to some forgotten god or hero of Anglo-Saxon times – an ancestor of the great Ray Barlow perhaps – who was venerated in this particular area of England, and whose 'grove' or sacred place, was at Bromsgrove. Possibly his court was at Bromyard, and the chief city was indeed Bromwycham. Which simply underlines the point that Bromwycham is indeed the capital of the Midlands which, as any fule kno, means West Bromwich is in fact, the centre of the universe. Don't let anybody tell you different.

CORNER OF THE WORLD

Few Albion managers have taken as much stick down the years as Ron Saunders. None can question the success that he enjoyed at Villa Park – in particular in the late 1970s and early 1980s – but once he left their employ, it was all downhill for him. Or was it? Some conspiracy theorists will argue that even after he left Witton, he remained in the employ of Mr Ellis and, given the way things went for him at Birmingham City, and then in God's country, it's a theory that has legs. But let's be honest, by the time Saunders arrived at The Hawthorns, Albion was a club in steep decline. From the glory days of the 1978/79 magicians, we had hit the skids and we were hurtling towards Division Two – that's the Championship kids – and the prospect of anybody saving us was slim. There were costs to cut, wage bills to trim, and a club to rebuild. On the face of it, the board's appointment of Saunders made a degree of sense. His Villa pedigree was unquestionable and as a no-nonsense organiser, there were few to compare with him. And Albion were a team that needed organising, for while we had talent – Derek Statham, Garth Crooks, Mickey Thomas, Steve Mackenzie, Jimmy Nicholl to name but a few – we were slumped at the bottom of the table. We might not have been quite dead, but there was a plot in the graveyard with our name on it.

Given his granite-faced demeanour and his somewhat cadaverous look, the sardonic Saunders might not be the first person you'd think of when looking for someone to administer the kiss of life. Exhumations, yes. Resurrections? Perhaps, no. The tales of the players of the time are legion. Playing devil's advocate, Saunders had a massive job to do and absolutely no time to do it in. As he made clear, he wasn't there to be the people's friend. He was there to do a job and knock the football club into shape. Whether his approach was the right one is a moot point. Certainly the post-Saunders years saw Albion spiral further and further down, slipping into lower and lower circles of hell that not even Dante had imagined. Not that it was much fun for some players while he was here, not least those that didn't live within five minutes reach of The Hawthorns. That covered pretty well all the experienced pros, the ones who might have dug us out of trouble but who found themselves ostracised, banned from the main dressing room, and generally treated as pariahs. Right or wrong, one thing we can say with certainty; it didn't get us the results we needed, nor did it ever threaten to.

One nugget from that first 1985/86 season says pretty much everything about the relationship Saunders had with his senior players. Out on the training field, the Throstles of the day were indulging in a practice match as a rare treat from running up and down the outsides of blocks of flats as per the demands of the regime. Back from injury was Gary Owen, cultured midfielder, neat and tidy passer of the football. As was his wont, Gary was making himself available for the ball and then passing it short, keeping things moving. 'Tippy' was not the style that Mr Saunders wanted to embrace, never mind 'tappy'. A shrill blast on the whistle brought proceedings to a sudden halt. "Bottom of the table. You know why we're bottom of the table? Because that's how you play your football. Next time you get the ball facing our goal, I want you to hook it out over there, 60 yards forward and out wide so that we can chase it down and get nearer their goal. Get it out by the corner flag." Another blast on the whistle and the game resumes. After a few moments, the ball reaches Gary Owen in the centre circle, back to goal. For those of you too young to recall him, he was some player was Gary Owen, a beautiful passer of the ball, a purveyor of raking passes from one side of the field to the other. So, he took the ball down on his chest and without a look, clips the ball over his shoulder, passing it fully 60 yards. Second bounce, it hits the corner flag. Like finding half a needle in a field of haystacks. Then threading a camel through it. A source of the time says that all was still for a brief second as everyone looked across to the manager. The self same source swears that he could see the manager making internal calculations. Was that an accident? Was Owen really that good? Did he do that deliberately? Is he taking the mick? Let's just say that Gary Owen's Albion career did not last long thereafter.

KEEPING IT IN THE FAMILY

Albion has long had a reputation as something of a family club. Generally, that refers to the way in which supporters are welcomed into the fold and, in particular, the way the Baggies tradition is passed down the ages. But that's not limited to the fans, for on the pitch, too, the Throstles have reason to be grateful to a number of family dynasties who have served the club well.

Ronnie and Russell Allen – father and son
Ronnie was the supreme centre forward, one of the finest all-round strikers in the game's history. He joined Albion from Port Vale back in March 1950 and went on to amass 415 first-team appearances for the club, scoring 234 goals, including two in the 1954 FA Cup Final as the Baggies beat Preston North End 3-2. Allen also represented England on several occasions. His son, Russell, had limited opportunities at Albion after signing in the early 1970s, playing youth and reserve team football.

George and Harry Bell – cousins
George, an outside left, was a professional with Albion between 1878 and 1885 and amassed over 150 games for the Baggies prior to the inception of the Football League in 1888, scoring over 50 goals, including the winner in the 1883 Staffordshire Cup Final against Stoke. Cousin Harry, a full-back, was on Albion's books from the very start in 1879, a product of the George Salter Works. He made over 100 appearances prior to league football, with 14 FA Cup games to his name before he retired through injury in 1887.

Sidney and William Bowser – brothers
Sid was a talented inside-forward who was equally at home at centre-half; he took a mean penalty to boot. He was a member of the championship-winning side of 1920, gained a promotion medal in 1911, and an FA Cup runners-up medal in 1912. His 72 goals in 371 appearances for the Baggies make him an Albion legend. Brother Bill only had one first-team appearance to his name, but in two years at the club, turned out over 30 times for the second string.

Bruce and Ian Collard – brothers
Ian joined the club as a junior in 1962 and worked his way through the ranks to become a vital cog in Albion's 1968 FA Cup-winning team. He moved to Ipswich Town in May 1969 in a swap deal involving Danny Hegan after making 97 appearances for Albion, scoring eight goals. Brother Bruce, despite spending four years at the Hawthorns, between 1969 and 1973, never made the jump from reserve-team football to the first team.

James and Adam Chambers – brothers
The only pair of twins to represent the club throughout its history. James was a talented full-back who has continued to play at Championship level after leaving Albion after 80 first-team games. Brother Adam played a crucial part in midfield in the promotion-winning season of 2001/02 before a series of back injuries wrecked his Albion career.

George and Joseph Dorsett – brothers
George was a Second Division championship winner with Albion in 1902 and overall he scored 22 goals in 100 first-team outings before moving on to Manchester City in 1904. Brother Joe, also a winger, scored three goals in 18 appearances, before also joining Manchester City and actually playing in the same City side as George.

Jimmy and George Dudley – brothers
Jimmy was an enormously talented wing-half, who was a member of the 1953/54 'Team of the Century', gaining both an FA Cup winners, and a First Division runners-up, medal with Albion. After 15 years' service and 320 first-team appearances for the Throstles, Jimmy left The Hawthorns for Walsall before eventually retiring in 1967. Elder brother George joined Albion as a pro in 1937, and spent nine years at the club, mainly in the reserves. He did, however, score nine goals in 25 appearances, before moving on to Bromsgrove Rovers in 1946.

Thomas Charles and Thomas Green – father and son
Tommy Green was an inside forward with Albion between 1885 and 1887, when he joined Aston Villa. In his time with the Baggies, he scored eight goals in 16 first-team outings, including two losing FA Cup finals in 1886 and 1887. His son, Tommy Green junior, spent two years at Albion from May 1894, before moving on to Small Heath.

John Henry and Ezra Horton – brothers
The footballing Horton brothers both joined Albion as amateurs in 1882, and both turned pro in 1885; John, a full-back and Ezra, a wing-half. Between them they made over 200 first-team appearances for the club. John retired in 1899, after 17 years at Albion, and remained a Baggies fan until he passed away in 1946. Ezra retired in 1891.

George and Roland William James – brothers
George James was a prolific goalscoring centre forward, netting 57 times in 116 appearances for the club. Joining Albion in 1920, he eventually left the club after nine years, for Reading in May 1929. His brother, Roland, was at The Hawthorns at the same time as George, but this workmanlike wing-half had limited opportunities in the first team, turning out only nine times before moving on to Brentford in 1922.

George and Michael Lee – father and son
George 'Ada' Lee, was a member of the cup-winning team of 1954 and provided the cross from which Ronnie Allen put the Baggies a goal up in that game. A talented and very underrated winger, he joined Albion from Nottingham Forest for a then substantial fee of £7,500. George scored 65 goals in 295 outings in the first team. He later returned as trainer/coach in 1959, before moving to Norwich City in the same role in 1963, remaining with the Canaries until retirement in 1987. Son Michael joined Albion as an amateur in 1956, but never really made the grade, making only one first-team appearance, against Sheffield Wednesday in December of that year. A Welsh schoolboy and youth international, he also netted 12 goals in 45 Central League outings, featuring alongside his father for Albion on a couple of occasions.

Hubert and Harold Pearson – father and son
Perhaps the greatest Albion dynasty and the most famous father and son goalkeeping double act in the game. Between them, they amassed 680 appearances as custodians in their combined careers at The Hawthorns. Father Hubert took over the reins from Jim Stringer, in the 1909/10 season, and eventually relinquished the role to son Harold in 1927. In August 1937, Harold was transferred to Millwall, which signalled the end of the Pearson era. Between them they achieved just about every award possible in the sport, including a championship medal for Hubert, and an FA Cup winner's medal and an England cap for Harold.

Jack, John William and William Paddock – father and sons
Jack Paddock was a trainer/coach, a self made man, and a true character who looked after the first team in the late 1890s into the early 1900s. Jack's two sons, John William and William, both wingers, both made the grade at Albion, though John William was the more successful, making a total of 31 first-team appearances, whilst brother Bill had only a handful, being forced to retire through injury and illness in 1888. He did, however, play for Albion in the 1887 FA Cup Final.

James Henry and James Thomas Pemberton – brothers
Jim Pemberton signed for the Albion as an amateur in September 1937, signing pro the following year. He was a member of the promotion-winning team that took the Baggies back to the big time in 1949. A virtual ever-present in the first post-war league campaigns, he was seriously injured against Villa in the opening fixture of the 1950/51 season, and never played again. Brother James Thomas, in contrast, only appeared in one first-team match for Albion, against Nottingham Forest in the Midland Cup in 1944. After leaving Albion, he forged a very useful career with Luton Town, making over 100 appearances for the Hatters.

Charles, Thomas and Walter Perry – brothers
Charles, captain of Albion and an England international, was arguably the most prominent of the trio. Appearing in four FA Cup finals in 1886, 1887, 1888 and 1892, he also won three England caps and two Football League XI caps. After retiring with 219 first-team appearances post 1888, and another 280 appearances pre-1888 to his name, he became a club director until 1902, overseeing the move to The Hawthorns. Thomas, an accomplished half-back, also served Albion loyally for ten years, amassing 291 appearances and 15 goals. He gained one England cap in 1898, and played three times for the Football League XI. Brother Walter had two spells with Albion but never really made the grade in either. He did score seven goals in 15 first-team outings. He later became reserve-team manager at Albion, before becoming a Football League linesman.

Cyrille Regis and Jason Roberts – uncle and nephew
Cyrille Regis burst on the scene in dramatic fashion in 1977, scoring goals 'Roy of the Rovers' would have been proud of, after his meteoric rise from non-league football with Hayes. Cyrille went on to score 112 goals in

over 300 appearances at The Hawthorns, before being sold, to the shock and horror of the fans, to Coventry City in 1984. Cyrille then went on to enjoy great careers there and at Villa and Wolves, cementing himself in the Midlands 'Hall of Fame'. Cyrille also returned to The Hawthorns for a spell on the coaching staff. Cousin Jason joined Albion from Bristol Rovers for £2 million in 2000. In three years at The Hawthorns – before his move to Portsmouth, on loan, and then Wigan Athletic – he scored 27 goals in 101 appearances. He also scored against Walsall on the day Albion fans gathered to mourn the passing of Jeff Astle, removing his shirt in celebration to reveal a T-shirt bearing Astle's picture beneath.

Bryan and Gary Robson – brothers
Bryan Robson, along with Cyrille Regis, Derek Statham, Ally Robertson, John Wile, Laurie Cunningham, Brendon Batson, Tony and Ally Brown, was an integral member of the Albion side of the late 1970s that enthralled crowds up and down the land. Joining Albion as an apprentice in 1972, Bryan turned pro in 1974, and never looked back. In his time at The Hawthorns, he amassed 249 first-team appearances and scored 46 goals, despite breaking his leg three times. Brother Gary had to live in the shadow of his famous brother, but nevertheless went on to give sterling service to the Baggies in his 12-year career at the club. Appearing in 256 first-team games at The Hawthorns, he netted 34 times, and also had the misfortune to break his leg, in the FA Cup fifth-round tie with Aston Villa at The Hawthorns.

Abraham Jones and Teddy Sandford – uncle and nephew
Abraham Jones, a Tipton lad, was a powerful centre-half, who joined Albion in 1896. In his five-year stay at Albion, he netted ten times in 117 appearances. Nephew Ted Sandford, one of the youngest players to appear in the Albion first team, went on to become another Baggies legend. Scoring 75 times in 317 appearances, Teddy won both FA Cup winners, and losers, medals in the 1931 and 1935 cup finals. He also won international honours, gaining one cap against Wales in 1932. After retirement, he returned to the club as a coach and scout between 1950 and 1967.

Arthur Reginald, Edward and William Smith – brothers
The three brothers all played for Albion in the late 1890s and early 1900s. Neither proved to be very prominent in the scheme of things

with William making the most appearances (22), scoring three goals. Arthur Reginald managed one goal in six first-team outings, and Edward four goals in ten appearances.

George Frederick and Samuel Wheldon – brothers
George Wheldon was signed from Aston Villa but after a one-year stay at the Albion, he was signed by Queens Park Rangers in December 1901. He was also an accomplished county cricketer with Worcestershire. Brother Sam was a pro at the Albion between 1891 and 1892, and only made one appearance for the club, against Accrington Stanley in a First Division fixture in January 1892. He was also reserve for Albion in the 1892 FA Cup Final.

TOP OF THE WORLD MA!

It's been over 30 years since Albion looked down at the rest of English footballing creation, the last occasion coming on January 13th 1979 when they drew 1-1 at Norwich City's Carrow Road, appropriately enough the beginning of the club's centenary year. It was a year of great expectations as Ron Atkinson's exciting team pursued trophies on three different fronts – First Division, FA Cup and Uefa Cup – and one where it seemed as if the Baggies were going to finally break through and join the country's elite in the chase for the glittering prizes. The fact that they had just broken the British transfer record by spending £516,000 on David Mills to bring him to The Hawthorns from Middlesbrough underlined the club's intentions, as did the fact that even then, Mills could only make the bench at Norwich. In many respects though, the Norwich game encapsulated the way the remainder of the season would go. Cyrille Regis gave a rampaging Albion the lead in the first period of the game but ill fortune struck them down in the second half, Martin Peters equalising as Albion were temporarily down to ten men, Brendon Batson awaiting the signal to return to the field after changing his boots. The Throstles' luck seemed to have changed irrevocably. Three weeks later, Albion were beaten 2-1 by Liverpool at Anfield to lose the leadership of the First Division and as fixtures piled up as the snow fell, the chance of winning the league had gone.

THE NEVER-ENDING STORY

A long time ago in a footballing galaxy far, far away, cup ties used to be decided by replays. Lots of them. Going on forever until one team fell, twitching, to the floor, finally gunned down by exhaustion. Penalty shootouts? Bah, a modern nonsense reserved only for Johnny Foreigner rather than the manly Brits...

The march of progress, and the way in which the Champions League in particular has swallowed up the footballing schedule, has consigned games played to the death to the history books, but the Throstles have been through their share of cup ties that have required a third game to settle matters – 15 of them in all. But the daddy of all Albion cup ties came in the 1952/53 FA Cup campaign when the Throstles were pitted against Chelsea in the fourth round. A Johnnie Nicholls goal at Stamford Bridge saw the tie brought back to The Hawthorns, but that ended goalless. A second replay was held at Villa Park, Jimmy Dudley scoring in a 1-1 draw before the teams headed for Highbury. Back in the capital, Chelsea hit form and hit four, Albion unable to replay. The four cup ties were played within the space of 12 days, the Throstles also beating Manchester City in the league during that time. Albion got their revenge over the Blues in the following year, drawing Chelsea in round three and winning 1-0 at The Hawthorns courtesy of an own goal from future West Ham United and England boss Ron Greenwood. That set the Throstles on the way to their fourth FA Cup victory, ultimately beating Preston 3-2 in the final. This is the only time Albion have played five consecutive cup ties against one club.

It's not that unusual for the Baggies to play the same team in the FA Cup in consecutive seasons though – it's happened on 13 different occasions. The first was in 1884/85 and 1885/86 when Blackburn Rovers were twice the Albion's opponents, the second time in the final itself, Rovers winning out in a replay. Blackburn are the only club who have been consecutive season opponents twice because it happened again in 1890/91 and 1891/92. Ironically, Albion also played Sheffield Wednesday in both of those seasons. The most recent example came in 2007/08 and 2008/09 when we played Peterborough United and came out on top in both years.

On two occasions, we've been paired with the same club three years running – Preston North End from 1886/87 to 1888/89 and Aston Villa from 1923/24 to 1925/26. In sharp contrast, the longest gap between cup ties is 119 years 342 days, between the 1889 meeting with Burnley and the one in 2009. We were so glad to see them again, we promptly had a replay and went up to Turf Moor – and lost.

THE FULL SET

Graham Williams is one of the greatest club servants in Albion's history, as both player and captain. With over 350 appearances to his name, Graham did the lot for Albion, including completing a unique set as the only Throstle to play in the FA Youth Cup final, the Football League Cup Final, the FA Cup Final and the FA Charity Shield. After signing for Albion as a youngster from Rhyl, Graham began his footballing odyssey in the FA Youth Cup as part of the side that was brushed aside by the might of Manchester United's Busby Babes in the competition of 1955, Albion losing the final 7-1 on aggregate, Williams playing as a winger. Eleven years later, Graham was a crunching full-back and a leader of men as he took his side into battle in the two-legged League Cup final against West Ham, the Throstles coming through against Moore, Hurst, Peters et al to win 5-3 over the two games, Graham getting one of the goals.

He and the Albion almost repeated the feat a year later as they marched to the League Cup final again beating West Ham in a two-legged semi-final this time, before pitching up at Wembley for the final against Third Division Queens Park Rangers. Albion were cruising at 2-0 up at half-time but contrived to lose the game 3-2. Vowing to make amends, Albion were back at Wembley the following season, this time in the FA Cup Final where Graham realised a boyhood dream by captaining the winning side and going up the famous Wembley steps to collect the FA Cup. As a result, the Baggies were involved in the following season's curtain raiser, the Charity Shield, played at the home of the champions, Manchester City. City were imperious, winning 6-1, helped by the fact that Albion goalkeeper John Osborne was injured and had to go off. His replacement between the sticks? Graham Williams.

KEYS TO THE HAWTHORNS

One of the most important influences on the early history of West Bromwich Albion was Mr Harry Keys, an early director of the club, at the time of those last difficult days at Stoney Lane, Albion's ground before the move to The Hawthorns. Harry took over the chairmanship from T. H. Spencer, at the annual general meeting held on June 30th 1899 and took over leadership of the club at a most crucial time in its existence. Famously nicknamed 'John Bull' by the players, Harry created an early dynasty at the club, with brothers W. Hall Keys, and Clement Keys, who held positions as director, and secretary, respectively. Continuing the dynasty, his son Major H. Wilson Keys, joined the Albion board on his father's death in 1929 becoming chairman himself in 1947. He held that role until 1963, making it the second longest reign as chairman after Billy Bassett.

Harry was a dominant man with a forthright attitude, which led secretary Fred Everiss to proclaim; "He was a man who called a spade a spade, and sometimes a sanguinary shovel." Having said that, he was also a warm man who endeared himself to generations of Albion footballers, and staff. Born on the Isle of Wight in March 1861, Harry came to West Bromwich at the tender age of three, was educated in Handsworth, and from an early age was an avid sportsman. His first love was cycling, winning many trophies and accolades, eventually becoming president of the Midland Cycling and Athletic Club. He also played football for Sandwell Road FC and became a big Albion fan, along with his father, councillor Samuel Keys. Always immaculately dressed, he was often attired in white spats, with of course the customary 'colourful bloom' in his lapel, a symbol of his keen interest in flowers. A superb artist, his sketches of animals, notably dogs, were renowned amongst his many friends and associates, who were sent copies of his work as presents, especially at Christmas time.

His first 'stint' as chairman came to an abrupt end in 1903, when his public disagreements with other members of the board, led to his resignation. Jem Bayliss took over at the helm, but the events leading up to the financial crisis and the 'Shilling Fund' appeal in 1905 saw Harry re-instated as chairman, with the backing of Billy Bassett. With the club finally back on a sound financial footing, Harry stood down once again, with Bassett taking over. In his time at the Albion's helm, Harry extended his presence and influence throughout the football world, and was elected to the Football League Management Committee in 1905. In 1910, his contribution was recognised when he was elected vice-president of the Football League, an honour he held until his death. He also received a long service medal for his 21 years' service on the management committee. An amazing man, he was also a leading figure in local football, becoming president of the Staffordshire Football Association, and vice-president of both the Birmingham & District Football League and the Birmingham Works Football Association. In 1918, he became a member of the Football Association Council and the International Selection Committee, following on from his valuable work during the 1914-18 conflict, when he was a member of the Administration Committee appointed to manage the football war fund.

Probably his greatest hour as chairman was to oversee the club's transfer from Stoney Lane to The Hawthorns in 1900. It was he who had been tasked with finding a new site and discovered the barren piece of land at the corner of the Birmingham Road and Halfords Lane, which was owned at that time by the Sandwell Park Colliery Company. Negotiations completed, the green light for the move was given by the board on his recommendation at their meeting on January 30th 1900.

COME IN NUMBER 11, YOUR TIME'S UP!

On April 20th 1963, Albion played West Ham United at The Hawthorns, the fourth game in eight days as they struggled to cope with a fixture backlog. On the morning of the game, Clive Clark had to pull out of the game due to his wife being ill. The obvious replacement was Geoff Carter but, unfortunately, Geoff was playing against Leeds United reserves at Elland Road and the coach had already left – this in the era where ordinary phones were exotic enough, never mind mobiles. With the assistance of the police, the club issued an SOS message via the morning radio programme, which amazingly the reserve players were tuned in to. The message; "Will the driver of the West Bromwich Albion team coach, on the way to Leeds, please pull over and contact the police," was duly acted upon and manager Jimmy Hagan made his way north to intercept the coach and pick up Carter. Back at the Hawthorns, skipper Don Howe had assumed responsibility for the team in Hagan's absence and started re-arranging the team, not knowing if Carter would get back in time. With minutes to go, Carter made the Hawthorns and all was well as the Throstles won by the only goal of the game, scored by Alec Jackson.

THE GREENHOUSE EFFECT

Have you heard the one about the Scotsman, the Black Countryman and the greenhouse? Hold on, it's a belter, believe me, and all a part of the rich tapestry of the career of Willie Johnston, perhaps the single most entertaining footballer ever to play for the Throstles.

"My philosophy was always that the fans pay good money to come and watch you so it's up to you to go out there and entertain them and give them something for their money," said Willie. "A lot of times I ended up taking the mickey out of defenders just to get the crowd going, but I was still trying to do my job for the football team as well, help us score goals. But I don't see why that means you can't entertain them at the same time. Big Ron Atkinson was ideal for that attitude because before a game he'd always say; 'Willie, go out and do something stupid.' I used to try and trap the ball with my backside and I did it the one time in front of Brian Clough and he went berserk. He didn't like it, he thought it was unprofessional, but that was part of the game. I came out with a clown's mask on before the one game and there was uproar. What's the problem – I took it off before we started playing!"

So then, the greenhouse. What's that all about? "I always used to take the corner kicks here and I heard this guy shouting at me, right down the front, and he always talked about gardening and I liked to garden. So we go having a chat game after game, and the one week, he was talking about a greenhouse.

"He said, 'I believe you're looking for a greenhouse Willie?' Which I was at the time. So he said; 'I've got one for sale if you want it.' So I was taking the corner and so I said; 'Wait 'til the next corner and I'll speak to you.' So we got another corner down there and he told me that he wanted 50 quid for it. 'No, I'm not paying that kind of money for it.' So this went on for two or three games but I eventually got the greenhouse off him just through taking the corner kicks!"

HAT-TRICK HEROES

Knocking in a hat-trick is the height of the goalscorer's art, the modern-day reward being the opportunity to take the matchball home. The Throstles have had plenty of hat-trick heroes down the years, and here are the top ten:

W.G.Richardson 14
(he added nine more in wartime fixtures)
Ronnie Allen 9
Tony Brown.. 9
Jimmy Cookson.. 9
Derek Kevan... 8
Jeff Astle.. 7
Lee Hughes 5
Tom Pearson.. 5
Fred Shinton.. 5
Ike Clarke 4
(he scored five more in wartime fixtures)

A further 22 players have registered two or more hat-tricks, with another 33 scoring just the one. Of those 33, Billy Elliott scored seven more hat-tricks during the war, and Harry Jones knocked in six more. Len Millard – better known as a defender when he collected the FA Cup as captain in 1954 – also scored two hat-tricks, both during the war. Horace Ball and Peter McKennan both scored a single wartime hat-trick each. And spare a thought for Eric Jones who scored a hat-trick against Tottenham in a game in September 1939 that was declared null and void, so it didn't count. There again, that disappointment probably paled into insignificance when set against the reason why – football was halted for the duration when World War II broke out the day after the game. Derek Kevan's eighth and last hat-trick for the club came in the 6-1 demolition of Ipswich Town on March 9th 1963. Within the week, he'd been sold to Chelsea, either as reward or punishment, nobody is quite sure. Albion's only Premier League hat-trick to date was scored by Robert Earnshaw in the 4-1 win at Charlton Athletic during the 'Great Escape' of 2004/05, a feat that helped turn Albion's ailing season around. Tony Brown scored the Baggies' only European hat-trick thus far, against DOS Utrecht in the 5-2 second-leg win at The Hawthorns in the second round of the Inter-Cities Fairs Cup in 1966/67.

AWAY FROM IT ALL

Pre-season tours, mid-season breaks, post-season tours, they are all part of the fabric of life for footballers these days, especially at Premier League and Championship level. But even back in the mists of time, English clubs were ready to take the footballing gospel across the globe, the Baggies first taking the air in foreign climes as far back as 1909 when they headed to Scandinavia. Something of a marathon, it took in seven games in May 1909 and saw Albion take on the natives as well as fellow British tourists. They lost 3-0 to Newcastle United, beat Geffe FC 10-0 and triumphed over a Stockholm XI, 8-3. There were two games against Hull City, winning 2-1 and losing 4-3. The final two matches were against a Danish XI, which was lost 3-1, followed by a 2-0 win over a Swedish XI.

Albion did not tour again until the May of 1946, when they took in a short three-match tour of Belgium and Luxembourg. The first game against a Belgium XI ended in a 5-4 defeat, whilst the following match saw Albion defeat a Fola Jennesse XI 5-1. The final match, against Anderlecht, ended all square at 1-1. Seven years later, the 'Team of the Century', destined to come so close to the league and FA Cup double, undertook a short tour of Ireland in May 1953. The first match against Talgarth Juniors was won 2-0. Albion then completed the tour with wins against Waterford, 5-4, and Bohemians, 5-1. Then came the ground-breaking three-match tour of the Soviet Union in 1957 and an unbeaten campaign it was too. The first match against Zenit was drawn 1-1, and the two other matches, against Dynamo Tbilisi, and the Red Army were won 3-1 and 4-2, respectively. Two years later Albion were off on a physically demanding nine-match tour of Canada and the United States. Dundee United were familiar opponents out there; three games played, one drawn 2-2, the Throstles winning the other two 7-1 and 4-2. The Ontario All Stars were thumped 6-1, but that was just a warm-up for beating the Alberta All Stars 15-0. A Manitoba Select side were brushed aside 10-1, and a Canadian XI were beaten 9-0. The two other matches in the campaign were a 4-0 win against Montreal All Stars, and the only defeat of the tour, 3-2 against British Columbia. Albion's overall record on the trip was played 9, won 7, drawn 1, lost 1, scored 59, conceded 10.

In May 1961, Albion embarked on a short tour of Austria where a 3-3 draw against Lustenau was followed by wins against Linz 3-2 and Graz 2-1. Three years later, in August 1964, Albion went to Holland where they were defeated 2-1 by AZ Alkmaar, but managed wins against ADO 2-1 and a tremendous victory against Ajax, 1-0, with Bobby Hope grabbing the winner. In July 1965, manager Jimmy Hagan took his team to the searing heat of New York to take part in a four-team international tournament. Albion would be pitting their skills against Kilmarnock from Scotland, Ferencvaros from Hungary and Polonia Byton from Poland. The first game against Kilmarnock ended in a surprising 2-0 defeat, and the tournament pretty much went downhill from there. Successive draws against Ferencvaros, 1-1, and Byton, 2-2, gave Albion a slim chance of qualifying for the final, in the round-robin tournament. A 2-0 win against Kilmarnock boosted the side's chances, but successive defeats against Ferencvaros, 2-1, and Polonia 6-0, ensured Albion were on their way home to a much more agreeable climate.

In May and June 1966, Albion embarked on a South American sortie comprising of six matches. Albion beat Alianza Lima 3-2 and Sporting Crystal 2-1, before drawing the third match of the tour 1-1 against a Uruguay XI. The next match against Newell's Old Boys was drawn 0-0, before the fifth game against a Uruguay select side ended in the only defeat of the campaign, 2-0. The final match against a Flamengo XI got the Baggies back into winning ways, 2-1. In May and June 1968, the victorious FA Cup-winning side took on yet another ground-breaking assignment, this time to the dust and the heat of East Africa. The first two matches of a 'fractious' tour were drawn, 1-1 against Dar-es-Salaam, and 1-1 against Tanzania. The third match, against a Ugandan XI was won 1-0, and followed by another victory against the Kenyan national side 2-1. Albion then drew 2-2 against East Africa and finished the tour on a winning note with a 4-3 victory over the Kenyan national side again. The penultimate fixture against East Africa, in Kampala, ended with an unseemly encounter. Many of the players who had taken part in the tour remarked on how the hosts, being of the opinion that they were in fact playing against the England team, ensured the games were a little less than friendly. Fortunately, the dismissals of Graham Williams and Asa Hartford were not carried over to the start of the new season.

In May 1969, Albion went back to Canada and the USA, a tour that included the three-match Palo Alto tournament. Albion opened the campaign with two wins against Vancouver All Stars, 2-0, and Victoria O'Keefes, 4-1. Albion beat Dukla Prague 2-1 in the first match of the Palo Alto tournament, followed by a 2-2 draw against California Clippers. The final match against Setubal was lost 1-0, which ended Albion's participation. The final game against Edmonton All Stars was won 12-0, with goals from Dennis Martin, Bobby Hope, Danny Hegan, Graham Lovett, John Kaye, Dick Krzywicki and Len Cantello. In July that year, just before the start of the new season, Albion engaged in a short two-match tour of Norway, with mixed results – a 3-2 defeat at the hands of a Norway under-23 select XI, and an emphatic victory over SK Lyn of Oslo, 6-0. The following year in May 1970, Albion took part in the Anglo-Italian Tournament for the first time. Home games against Lanerossi Vincenza and AS Roma, were drawn 0-0 and won 4-0, respectively, with the away games both being drawn 1-1. Unfortunately, the away leg against AS Roma was abandoned after 76 minutes, when fighting broke out between players, fans and officials. The following May, Albion entered the tournament again and played games against Inter Milan and Cagliari. Both games at The Hawthorns were drawn 1-1, and both away fixtures, in the June, ended with 1-0 defeats.

In May 1972, Albion went to Yugoslavia, to play three matches against Hajduk Split (lost 2-1), FK Velez (won 3-2) and finally FK Sarajevo (drew 1-1). Two months later, in July and August, Albion went to Sweden to play Kalmar (won 3-0), Helsingborg (won 3-1), and Lanskroner (drew 1-1). During that season Albion also played two away friendly fixtures against Feyenoord in Holland, which they lost 4-1, and Hibernian in Scotland, winning 2-0. In July 1974, the Baggies popped over to Belgium for two matches against FC Mechelen and Diest. Albion lost the first match 1-0, but beat Diest 2-1. Then in July 1975, after the arrival of Johnny Giles, Albion embarked on another short tour, this time to Ireland. Shamrock Rovers were beaten 1-0, and Finn Harps got the better of Albion by the same scoreline. In 1977, Albion warmed up for the new campaign, with an appearance in the Tennent Caledonian Cup at Ibrox, beating St. Mirren in the semi-final, 4-3, and Rangers in the final, 2-0. They then jetted off to Alicante in Spain, to play in the Trofeo Costa Blanca, beating Dynamo Tbilisi 1-0, and crashing to Hercules Pegasus, 5-1. That December, just before Christmas, they flew over to Dhahran to play a Saudi Arabian XI, a Tony Brown goal wrapping up the 1-0 win.

At the end of that 1977/78 season, they embarked on probably the most momentous trip yet, to China. Five matches, five wins and 16 goals says it all as far as the playing front is concerned, but it really was much more than that. Albion were very much pawns in the FA's attempt at glasnost with the emerging world giant. Not one playing member of the side has actually said that it was an enjoyable tour, but most have admitted it was educational. For the record, Albion beat a Peking XI 3-0, a China XI 2-0, Shanghai 2-0, Kwangtung Province 6-0 and finally a Hong Kong XI 3-0. That August, Albion went to Syria and played two matches against a National Province XI – which they won 1-0 – and the Damascus Police, which ended all square at 1-1. Albion also competed a week earlier, in the Tennent Caledonian Cup again, going out of the competition thanks to a 2-0 defeat at the hands of Hearts.

In May 1979, a Danish tour of three matches comprised of defeat at the hands of Aalborg IF, 1-0, and victories over FUIN Boldspol, 4-1, and IHF Aarhus, 7-0. In August, Spain was again the venue for the Trofeo Teresa Herrera Tournament. However, defeats against Sporting Gijon and Honved, both 1-0, ended their participation. After Christmas, manager Ron Atkinson took the team to Bahrain for two matches in the sun. Both games were won, Al-Imarat beaten 3-0, and a Bahrain XI lost 4-1. In August 1980 Albion took part in the Trofej Marjan Tournament, held in Yugoslavia. However, an early departure was confirmed with a 5-1 defeat to Hajduk Split, followed by a 0-0 stalemate with FC Zurich. At the end of the season, in May 1981, Canada and the USA were again the venues for three matches against Vancouver Whitecaps (lost 2-1), Portland Timbers (won 1-0), and Edmonton Drillers (won 2-1). In August, just prior to the new season, the club enjoyed a successful tournament winning the Sevilla International Trophy in Spain by beating Real Betis 4-1, and Sevilla 2-0.

In August 1982, Spain again was the destination for the Barcelona International Tournament. Defeats against RCD Espanyol 3-2, and CA Osasuna 2-1, meant that Albion once again travelled home empty handed. In August 1983, a successful three-match unbeaten tour of

Holland was undertaken with wins over Den Bosch 3-0, and Go Ahead Eagles 4-3, along with a 2-2 draw with NAC Breda. That signalled a lull in overseas touring until the summer of 1989, when Albion embarked on an Irish tour in the July and August. Three matches – three wins; against Shelbourne 4-2, Cobh Ramblers 4-2, and Glentoran 3-2. At the end of the season, at the end of May 1990, Spain was again the venue, for the San Jose Cup. It was pretty disastrous. A 6-1 defeat at the hands of Real Madrid was followed by a rather better performance against Vasco Da Gama, Albion going down 4-2. From Spain, Albion went straight to the USA for two end-of-season matches against Arizona Condors and LA Heat. Comfortably accounting for Condors 6-1, Albion were held to a 1-1 draw by LA Heat. Just prior to the 1990/91 season, Albion went to Ireland once again for a four-match, unbeaten tour. Glentoran were held 0-0, Ards defeated 4-0, as were Newry Town 3-1, with the final match against Shelbourne being drawn 1-1.

Thereafter, for nearly a decade, home friendlies were preferred to perhaps the costlier foreign trips, until Albion embarked on a short two-match tour of Denmark in July 1999, under manager Brian Little, since which time the overseas training camp has become a stock part of pre-season preparation rather than a specific tour as in days of yore.

NOT NEEDED ON VOYAGE

Albion have often broken cultural and geographical boundaries with a variety of pioneering tours such as those to Scandinavia in 1909, Russia in 1957 and China in 1978.

The Throstles also travelled to East Africa in the immediate aftermath of the 1968 FA Cup Final, but they might have found themselves in that continent some 36 years earlier had they taken up the offer of a trip to South Africa. However, for reasons that were not divulged, the board of directors turned down the invitation and the tour was later offered to both Huddersfield Town and Arsenal.

I SHOULD BE SO LUCKY

Ray Fairfax had a distinguished career at The Hawthorns, both as a player and as a member of the Albion's administrative function after hanging up his boots, having played a crucial part in his role as a member of the team that won the Football League Cup in 1965/66, beating West Ham United 5-3 on aggregate. He also scored a single goal for the club, in an Inter-Cities Fairs Cup tie against Bologna, as Albion were beaten 3-1 at The Hawthorns. He had his share of luck off the pitch to when his numbers came up on the football pools. For years, he'd chosen the same numbers but one day, while driving, decided it was time for a change and picked some fresh ones off the radio dial. Shortly after, Ray came up with a first dividend which put him on football's rich list for winning what was little more than a weekly wage for some players today.

ENGLAND 4 WEST GERMANY 2 (ALBION 5)

1966 was, of course, the golden year for English football, the year when the World Cup was won, the West Germans were vanquished and Kenneth Wolstenholme's commentary became part of the nation's folklore. At the head of England's World Cup-winning team were three men from West Ham United. Bobby Moore, who skippered the side, lined up alongside Geoff Hurst and Martin Peters, who both scored the goals on that legendary day. They'd had a pretty good run given that West Ham won the FA Cup in 1964 and then the European Cup Winners' Cup a year later, but they were by no means invincible. In the League Cup competition for 1965/66, West Ham had maintained their great cup fighting tradition by battling their way through to what was then a two-legged final, played home and away, where the Albion were their opponents. The first game was at Upton Park and in a close fought encounter, the Hammers prevailed, winning 2-1. But back in the 1960s, going to play at The Hawthorns, especially under the lights, was a daunting prospect, for an attack-minded Albion feared nobody on home turf. Tony Brown recalls that; "We were that wound up for the game we were virtually kicking the dressing room door down to get out on the pitch and get at West Ham." Whatever manager Jimmy Hagan had been feeding his players, it did the trick as the Baggies swept West Ham aside in a blistering first-half display to eventually win the final 5-3 on aggregate and collect the trophy at the first attempt, Albion having refused to enter the competition in its opening years. But then West Bromwich were always better than West Germany.

FUDGE MIXES WITH THE TOFFEES

With Albion in mid-table as the 1963/64 season approached its close, a visit from top-of-the-table Everton was a game that offered real interest for supporters but also gave manager Jimmy Hagan an opportunity to experiment with his team. Playing with a re-shaped forward line due to an injury to John Kaye, Hagan drafted in 18-year-old Mick Fudge to play at inside-left, with Ronnie Fenton reverting to centre forward. Fudge had played for the reserves the previous day, against Aston Villa, in a game Albion lost 1-0, and by the manager's own words, had not had the best of games. Having made his debut against Sheffield United at the Hawthorns in December 1963, Fudge was on the score-sheet against Spurs in a Christmas 4-4 thriller but had had limited opportunities thereafter. He had plenty to prove on the final day of March 1964, but did the job with a hat-trick against the reigning champions. Unfortunately, this game will be remembered for less savoury reasons, for the fixture was one of several documented in a bribery allegation against Everton wing-half, Tony Kay, the result tainted amid tales of match fixing.

Ironically, Fudge ran out at the start of the game to jeers and cat-calls from The Hawthorns faithful but those that jeered beforehand were cheering at the end as Fudge left the pitch to a hero's reception to leave manager Hagan rubbing his hands with glee. "Can you beat that," he declared. "Young Fudge was shocking for the reserve side yesterday, I'm scraping the barrel with only five forwards to call on, so I've no choice at all – and we end up beating the champions and playing like this. Fudge is a good boy. He gets in position. He missed them with the reserves, but those were three beauties he got today." Albion went on to win the game 4-2 – Graham Williams got the other – and that knocked Everton completely off their stride, the Toffees ending up third in the First Division, five points behind the eventual champions, Bill Shankly's Liverpool.

Mickey Fudge's Everton hat-trick contributed to a total of five goals scored in 16 first-team appearances whilst at The Hawthorns. When Alan Ashman took over as manager in 1967, he was released from Albion and joined Exeter City. He also had spells at Wellington Town, Telford United, Kidderminster Harriers, Malvern Town and Brierley Hill, eventually retiring from the game in 1981.

THAT'S ENTERTAINMENT

Albion against Manchester United was traditionally one of the great fixtures on the calendar, before money put United in a very different world. The late 1960s and early 1970s was a particular golden era for the fixture, though, United's holy trinity of Denis Law, George Best and Bobby Charlton up against Albion's own religious icons Jeff Astle, Tony Brown and Bobby Hope. Between 1965/66 and 1972/73 there were eight meetings between the clubs at The Hawthorns, the Throstles winning five and drawing two, never failing to score at least two goals in a game and registering three or more on five occasions. United were handy as well, so much so that the eight games gave up 43 goals in total; 25 for Albion, 18 for United.

Not surprisingly, there were a few hat-tricks amid those goals and games, one for David Herd in a 4-3 win for the Red Devils in 1966 and one for Tony Brown in the 4-3 Albion win of March 1970. The other came in an extraordinary game on a Monday night at The Hawthorns on April 29th 1968, a game which Albion won 6-3, Jeff Astle netting three times – he added a second hat-trick two days later in a 3-1 win against West Ham United at The Hawthorns. Forty-eight hours prior to taking on Manchester United, the Throstles had booked their place in the FA Cup Final by beating Birmingham City 2-0 in the semi-final at Villa Park. Matt Busby's team were busy on cup business of their own, having just won the first leg of their European Cup semi-final against Real Madrid, 1-0 at Old Trafford. By the end of May, the Baggies had carried off the FA Cup by beating Everton 1-0 and United had become the first English winners of the European Cup, defeating Benfica 4-1. Both finals were held at Wembley. Pitch was alright.

WORLD CUP WONDERS

Of the ten outfielders who won the World Cup for England in 1966, only Ray Wilson failed to score a competitive goal against the Throstles. Alan Ball, in particular, loved playing Albion, scoring two hat-tricks against the Baggies for Everton and a Blackpool brace to boot. Martin Peters scored 17 goals against Albion in his career, including hat-tricks for West Ham United and Spurs. Ironically, Geoff Hurst scored his last league goal for the Albion against Charlton Athletic on September 20th 1975, and played his last league game against Plymouth Argyle on October 18th that year. Nobby Stiles was manager, assistant manager and youth team coach at The Hawthorns during the mid 1980s. And a word for the goalkeeper. Gordon Banks saved a rare Graham Williams penalty in the Albion versus Stoke game at the Victoria Ground in 1967. The game finished goalless. Graham was kept away from penalties after that.

BOUNCED

Albion famously won promotion to the top flight as champions of the Second Division in 1911 but two seasons earlier they'd come within a whisker of promotion only to be denied by goal average, the method of separating teams on equal points back then – goals for divided by goals against. Indeed, when Albion finished their league campaign on April 26th 1909 with a 2-1 defeat at Derby County, they were top of the pile, but challengers Tottenham and Bolton Wanderers still had games to play. Tottenham were first to play, two days later also at the Baseball Ground, aware that a point would take them into top spot. They duly managed a 1-1 draw which nudged them ahead of Albion on goal average. On the 30th, it was Bolton's turn, again against Derby County, this time at Burnden Park. Playing their third game against the top three inside five days, the exhausted Rams went to the slaughter, lost 1-0 and Bolton finished champions, Albion stuck in third place and missing promotion by 0.02 of a goal, at which point, thoughts turned back to a trip to Blackpool on November 28th 1909 when the Throstles came away with a 2-0 win, despite having a perfectly good goal chalked off by a myopic referee.

Hewitt, the Albion centre forward, struck what was described as a 'very fast shot' at the goal. The ball flashed past the goalkeeper, entered the net, but rebounded from the net support, but so confident was he that the goal had been scored, Albion's Billy Garrity, who himself was in a position where he could easily have tapped the rebound in, ignored the ball, and walked back to the centre-circle in readiness for the game to be restarted. The keeper himself picked the ball up and kicked it back to the centre of the pitch, obviously for the same reason, but much to everyone's surprise, the referee, Mr Hammond, cried 'Play on'. Astounded Albion players appealed to both the referee and linesman, but all protestations fell on deaf ears. The referee was of the opinion that the ball had struck the crossbar, and rebounded into play. At the time, the local press declared that: "It would have been hard lines for the visitors, had the disallowing of the goal affected the result of the game in any way." But when the points and the goals were totted up at the end of the season, had that one been given, it would have been Albion, not Spurs, who went up.

A SPECIAL TALENT REVISITED

Andy Johnson was always of a bizarre turn of mind. Normal dressing room pranks like putting Deep Heat in people's underwear and cutting up their socks was meat and drink to the greatest living Welshman, but Jono's imagination stretched further and wider than that. Among perhaps his finest moments was the day when, on his way in to training during a spell of injury, he decided to visit a pet shop specialising in reptiles, not to buy a snake but to take delivery of a bag of dead mice used as feed. While the rest of the players were out working, Jono collected up the car keys of those foolish enough not to have safely locked them away. Russell Hoult returned to find dead mice beneath the bonnet of his car, but the best was saved for Jonathan Greening, then driving a little Mini Cooper. He got in to the car only to find dead mice sellotaped to his steering wheel, an obstacle he duly removed. What he failed to notice was the row of them attached to the parcel shelf at the back, Greening driving off oblivious to the rodent cemetery affixed to his car. Andy always was a generous soul so when his kids were bored one day, he tried to entertain them. But no Xbox for the Johnson brood, oh no. Instead, he went out and bought them a couple of lambs to play with. The novelty soon wore off, however, and legend has it that they were soon bundled into a van – the lambs, not the kids – and the following morning a local farmer awoke to find his flock had increased to the tune of two. In a further bid to entertain the kids one Christmas, Jono found a reindeer from somewhere and left it tethered in the garden on Christmas Eve so he could prove to the kids that Santa had been. As he recited the tale in the dressing room on Christmas afternoon, one member of the group was unimpressed. "You never got a real reindeer did you? You just nailed some antlers to a donkey didn't you!" Can you guess who that was dear reader? 'Twas a real reindeer though, which captivated the children for all of 30 seconds until they unwrapped a bike and the beast slipped away. So if you see a bewildered reindeer roaming around Bromsgrove – or a donkey with blood pouring out of its antlers for that matter – keep it to yourself eh?

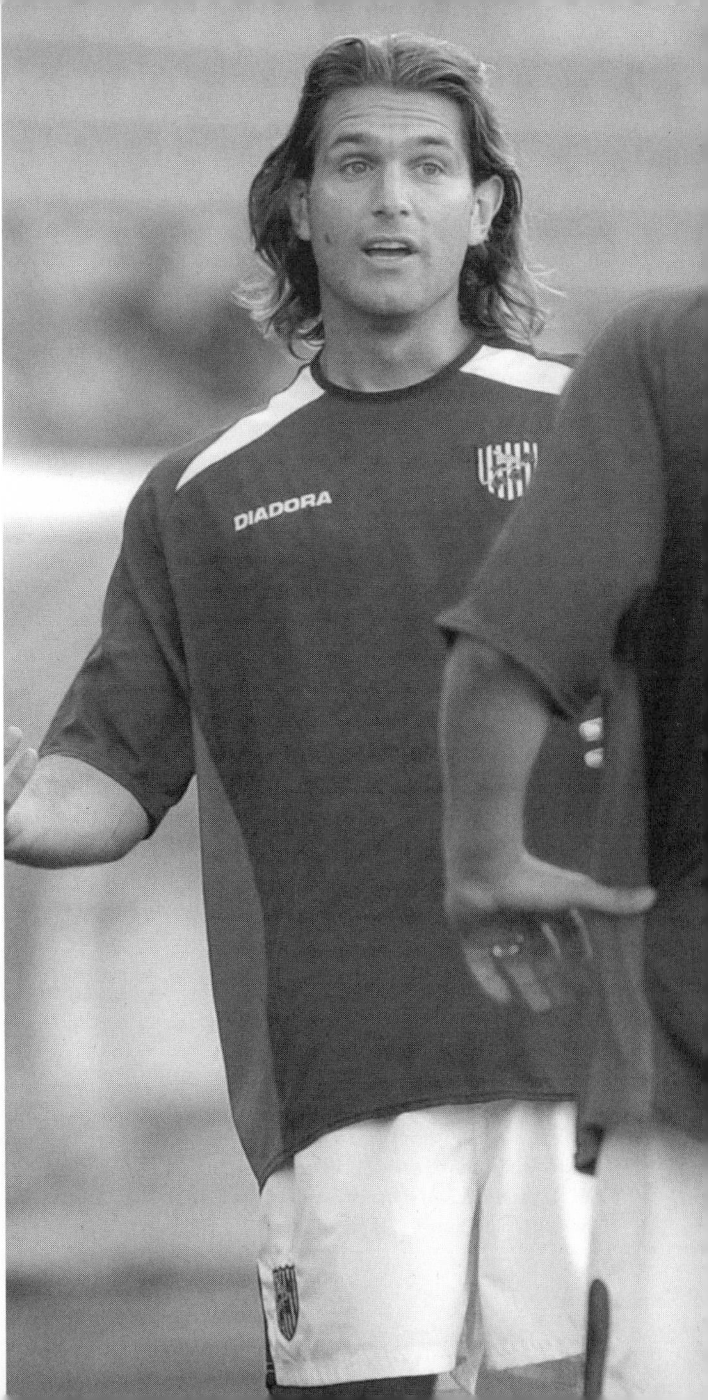

ANDY JOHNSON, PRACTICAL JOKER PAR EXCELLENCE

FOR CLUB AND COUNTRY

Albion have been fortunate enough to see many players turn out for their respective countries down the years, although it's only recently that a player has come from beyond the home nations and the Republic of Ireland. The global nature of modern-day football has completely changed that situation, of course, and over the last decade or so in particular, the Throstle gospel has been taken to the four corners of the earth as Albion men represent both club and country. Albion internationals, and their caps, are as follows – as at May 2nd 2010:

AUSTRALIA: Jason Van Blerk (4)
BELGIUM: Carl Hoefkens (4)
CANADA: Paul Peschisolido (9), Carl Valentine (1)
CAPE VERDE ISLANDS: Pedro Pele Monteiro (4)
CHILE: Gonzalo Jara (4)
CZECH REPUBLIC: Roman Bednar (2)
DENMARK: Martin Albrechtsen (1), Thomas Gaardsoe (2)
DUTCH ANTILLES: Shelton Martis (3)
ENGLAND: Albert Aldridge (1), Ronnie Allen (5), George Ashmore (1), Jeff Astle (5), Ray Barlow (1), Peter Barnes (6), Billy Bassett (16), Jem Bayliss (1), Sid Bowser (1), Wally Boyes (2), Tony Brown (1), Scott Carson (1), Joe Carter (3), Laurie Cunningham (3), Billy Elliott (2), Ben Garfield (1), Harry Hadley (1), Jack Haines (1), Don Howe (23), Steve Hunt (2), Derek Kevan (14), Harry Kinsell (2), Bobby McNeal (2), Tommy Magee (5), Fred Morris (2), Johnnie Nicholls (2), Harold Pearson (1), Jesse Pennington (25), Charlie Perry (3), Tom Perry (1), Joe Reader (1), Cyrille Regis (4), John Reynolds (3), W. G. Richardson (1), Stan Rickaby (1), Bob Roberts (3), Bryan Robson (13), Bobby Robson (20), Teddy Sandford (1), George Shaw (1), Joe Smith (3), Derek Statham (3), Billy Williams (6), George Woodhall (2)
HUNGARY: Zoltan Gera (31)
ICELAND: Larus Sigurdsson (12)
IVORY COAST: Abdoulaye Meite (9)
JAPAN: Junichi Inamoto (14)
MACEDONIA: Artim Sakiri (14)
NEW ZEALAND: Chris Wood (6)
NIGERIA: Nwankwo Kanu (13), Ifeanyi Udeze (2)
NORTHERN IRELAND: Gerry Armstrong (4), Chris Brunt (16), Danny Hegan (1), Jimmy Nicholl (11), James Quinn (15), Reg Ryan (1), Jack Vernon

(15), Dave Walsh (9), Paul Williams (1)

POLAND: Tomasz Kuszczak (2)

REPUBLIC OF IRELAND: Johnny Giles (7), Tony Grealish (10), Dean Kiely (3), Kevin Kilbane (10), Mark Kinsella (4), Mick Martin (10), Paul McShane (5), Paddy Mulligan (15), Joe Murphy (1), Reg Ryan (15), Ray Treacey (6), Dave Walsh (14)

ROMANIA: Gabriel Tamas (1)

SCOTLAND: Craig Beattie (3), Scott Dobie (6), Graham Dorrans (3), Doug Fraser (2), Asa Hartford (6), Bobby Hope (2), Willie Johnston (13), Derek McInnes (2), Sandy McNab (1), James Morrison (5), Nigel Quashie (3)

SENEGAL: Dio Kamara (17)

SLOVAKIA: Igor Balis (3), Marek Cech (10)

SLOVENIA: Bostjan Cesar (4), Robert Koren (24)

SOUTH KOREA: Do-heon Kim (7)

SWITZERLAND: Bernt Haas (12), Pascal Zuberbuhler (3)

WALES: Stan Davies (11), Billy Davies (2), Robert Earnshaw (11), Hugh Foulkes (1), Andy Johnson (8), Ivor Jones (4), Jason Koumas (21), Paul Mardon (1), Tony Millington (3), Jimmy Murphy (15), Seth Powell (4), Ronnie Rees (2), Walter Robbins (6), Mickey Thomas (2), Graham Williams (26), Stuart Williams (33), Doug Witcomb (9)

ON THE BUSES

When you've gone on to become one of the Albion's all-time legends, when you are remembered in a set of gates in your honour at the entrance to The Hawthorns on the Birmingham Road, and when your legion of fans simply refer to you as 'The King', it's hard to imagine that you could ever have been the victim of a case of mistaken identity. Yet on his arrival at the club, nobody had a clue just who this bloke Jeff Astle was. Signed from lowly Notts County by manager Jimmy Hagan on the morning of an Albion away game, he was hardly a household name and none of the Albion players had the slightest idea who he was or what he looked like. Astle was instructed to make his way to Filbert Street to meet his new teammates and get ready to make his debut for the Throstles. When Astle, who suffered from colour blindness, duly turned up in the Albion dressing room that night, clad in a bright green blazer, there was plenty of confusion amongst his colleagues at this interloper in their midst, until one of them said; "Are you the new bus driver mate? You can't come in here, you'll have to wait outside!" Fortunately, Jimmy Hagan arrived to make the appropriate introductions and, within a few games and a few goals, nobody ever wondered who Jeff Astle was ever again. The green blazer disappeared without trace though.

OUT OF AFRICA

Having won the FA Cup through Jeff Astle's goal against Everton at Wembley in 1968, Albion's season still wasn't over. End-of-season tours were very much the thing back in those days and the Baggies headed off for uncharted territory, playing games in Africa long before the likes of Nigeria and Cameroon had started to make waves on the world stage. It was an experience never to be forgotten, in every sense according to flying Welsh winger Dick Krzywicki.

"When we got out there, Alan Ashman, the manager said: 'I don't want anyone getting drunk, this is a serious trip, we're not here to muck about. We'll do some training tomorrow.' It was a trade mission tour or something, flying the flag, so they wanted us on our best behaviour, which was hard given we'd won the cup, the season was over and we wanted to wind down a bit. Anyway, this guy who was organising it, he said to me; 'Why don't you come out and I'll show you a few places around here.' We'd got nothing to do, so we said, 'Ok, off we go'. So we're going down the beach road, and this sports car, drop top, screams past us, stops at the side of the road and this gorgeous girl gets out, takes her clothes off and lies on the beach. This is a bit different to being in Smethwick! So then the guy says, 'Let's go and have a beer'. They were huge, these drinks. Me and Dennis Clarke had two bottles and we were gone! We got back to the hotel only to find the manager had called a meeting! I can remember standing up against this column in the room and as he's talking, I'm sliding down it! The lads were trying to hide me, so I got away with it!

"Alan then said he didn't want anybody sunbathing because we'd got a game coming up and the sun drains you. He was determined to win the games and put on a good show out there. But we never saw the sun at home so we sneaked up on to the roof, me, Jeff Astle, a couple of others – we thought he'd never know. But Jeff was wearing a string vest, sunbathing in that, so next day, we're in the dressing room, Jeff takes his shirt off and there's all these lines over his chest from the vest!"

BOMBER COMMAND

Any Albion fan worth his or her salt knows that Tony Brown is our record goalscorer, but where did the goals come from? Bomber certainly didn't discriminate over his career – he was perfectly happy to score goals against anybody. This is the all time list.

Arsenal 7, AS Roma 2, Aston Villa 10, Birmingham City 5, Blackburn Rovers 2, Blackpool 7, Bolton Wanderers 1, Bradford City 1, Bristol City 4, Bristol Rovers 1, Burnley 8, Cardiff City 1, Carlisle United 5, Charlton Athletic 1, Chelsea 12, Colchester United 2, Coventry City 14, Crystal Palace 1, Derby County 3, Dinamo Bucharest 2, DOS Utrecht 3, Everton 8, Fulham 4, Huddersfield Town 3, Hull City 1, Ipswich Town 9, Leeds United 8, Leicester City 5, Lincoln City 1, Liverpool 8, Luton Town 1, Manchester City 5, Manchester United 12, Millwall 1, Newcastle United 8, Northampton Town 2, Norwich City 2, Nottingham Forest 14, Notts County 6, Oldham Athletic 2, Oxford United 3, Peterborough United 5, Portsmouth 2, Preston North End 1, Queens Park Rangers 1, RFC Brugge 1, Scunthorpe United 2, Sheffield United 5, Sheffield Wednesday 4, Southampton 5, St. Mirren 2, Stoke City 6, Sunderland 12, Swindon Town 2, Tottenham Hotspur 12, Valencia 2, Walsall 2, Watford 1, West Ham United 10, Wolverhampton Wanderers 6, Wrexham 2, York City 1.

IT'S ONLY ROCK'N'ROLL...

There can't be many other clubs who've had two separate games sponsored by the rock elite, but Albion have. The first came on Tuesday 25th October 1977 when Led Zeppelin's drummer John Bonham sponsored the League Cup tie with Watford, though the Albion programme failed to cover itself in glory by welcoming the man who played on the 'stupendous hit Stairway To Superstars'. Still, at least that must have upset the Wolves-supporting Robert Plant every bit as much as his band-mate putting funds in the Albion's coffers. A little less than a year later and it was the turn of legendary guitarist Eric Clapton, then something of a regular at The Hawthorns, to sponsor a game. The I Shot The Sheriff hit-maker was the proud sponsor of Albion's Uefa Cup tie against Galatasaray on September 27th 1978. Both games were won by the Throstles which makes you wonder if the commercial department shouldn't be tapping up Dave Grohl or The Edge to sponsor a game some time soon.

THE TOP FORTY

Albion have been blessed with some great club men over the years, but only 40 have managed 300 or more games for the Throstles. This is the roll of honour:

Tony Brown	720
Len Millard	627
Alistair Robertson	626
John Wile	619
Jesse Pennington	496
Ray Barlow	482
Tommy Glidden	479
Joe Smith	474
Ronnie Allen	458
Joe Carter	451
W. G. Richardson	444
Tommy Magee	434
George Shaw	425
Stuart Naylor	420
Bobby Hope	403
Bobby McNeal	403
Joe Kennedy	397
Don Howe	379
Derek Statham	378
Daryl Burgess	377
Hubert Pearson	377
Bob Taylor	377
Sid Bowser	371
Len Cantello	369
Jeff Astle	361
John Kaye	361
Alistair Brown	359
Graham Williams	354
Clive Clark	353
Billy Elliott	330
Tony Godden	329
Jimmy Dudley	320
Freddie Buck	319

ALBION IN THE ORIENT

The world has changed very swiftly these last 30 years. The end of the Cold War, the demolition of the Berlin Wall and the collapse of the communist states, globalisation, the internet, all these things have served to open up the world, such that, perhaps North Korea and the most inhospitable corners of jungles, deserts and forests aside, nowhere on the globe is a complete mystery to us any longer. In 1978, however, not only was there the Iron Curtain to contend with but a Bamboo one too. China was a greater mystery still, more remote than the USSR, less welcoming to any foreign visitor, less tolerant of any dissenting voices. This was not the same China that just over a year ago played host to the Olympic Games. President Nixon and Prime Minister Heath had both ventured to China on diplomatic missions in the early 1970s but as ever, sport was on the agenda as a political weapon. The England team had been scheduled to go out there in the summer of 1978 to play some games but after the failure to qualify for the World Cup in Argentina the plan was shelved.

Albion chairman Sir Bert Millichip was also an influential FA committee man at the time and so his club stepped into the breach and jetted off to China in May 1978 in perhaps the most unusual club tour there has ever been. So trendsetting was the trip that not only did the nation's press get on the junket with them, but the BBC followed them too, the prestigious *The World About Us* filing a full scale, hour-long documentary about the jaunt. This was some coup in the days when *The World About Us* was second only to *Panorama* in the documentary stakes, and devoting an hour of prime time television to a football tour in the days of just three channels was unheard of. When the Beeb returned, they and the show's presenter Julian Pettifer had come back with some television gold in the form of *Albion In The Orient*, a real moment-in-time piece of filmmaking that not only captured a look at life in a country that would soon change forever, but also a look at a profession that was just about to be transformed.

The Albion players of the time were doing pretty well. FA Cup semi-finalists a month earlier, with the 'Three Degrees' of Brendon Batson, Cyrille Regis and Laurie Cunningham making waves among the first group of black players to make an impact on the English game, and with Ron Atkinson as manager they were a group that was suddenly in the limelight. Yet they were barely removed from the supporters who idolised them. The still lived in the local community, would have a pint where the supporters drank and while their earnings were better than average, they were still nothing special. There were few airs and graces about them, no sense that they should be kept apart from the rest of us, no star trips or tantrums. They were a bunch of 20-something, ordinary working-class blokes. Which perhaps did not make them best suited to a trip of cultural significance. Off camera, Irish international Mick Martin was so bored that he spent the trip entertaining the other players by reading out elaborate suicide notes that he was composing to send to his wife. A diplomatic incident was narrowly averted when an impromptu cricket match in their hotel grounds was halted by one side running up a white flag in surrender, apparently a horrible insult in China. And Sir Bert had to find a swift change of clothes when, in opening a door, he upset a bucket of water over himself, the contents having been meant for one of the other players.

On screen, things were watered down, but the same antipathy prevailed. Bryan Robson, then just a pre-England youngster, complained that the previous year the team had gone to Alicante, which had been a lot more fun because he liked sunbathing. Confronted by huge banquets, most of the Albion players scurried off to the table of English food, scorning the local nosh. Nowadays, it looks insensitive, but back in 1978, before we became blasé about foreign travel and other cultures, that insularity was simply an example of what each and every one of us would have done. Elder statesman Bertie Mee, on the trip as an FA representative, bemoaned the fact that few players went on the cultural excursions that had been set up for them, preferring instead to stay at the hotels. In their defence, this was the era of hardcore communist China where the players had no freedom to move around on their own and felt hemmed in by the situation. Many of the players on the trip have subsequently said that it was the worst they ever went on, more suited at the time to a week in Spain but now, as 50-somethings, they wish they could go back and do it again. Such is the way that youth is wasted on the young, as was the value of the experience.

As it is, the film is best remembered for one quote from midfielder John Trewick on the one trip that everyone went on – a visit to the Great Wall. Ron Atkinson later suggesting that; "I've bent free-kicks round bigger walls than this!" As part of a longer interview where Trewick talked about the impressive scale of it all, one quote was used: "You've seen one wall, you've seen them all." So if you want to know where the glorious art of footballers being stitched up started, and why they now prefer to say nothing, it's down to *The World About Us*. That aside, it's a truly fascinating film, both for its glimpses of sportsmen abroad, of communist China and for a world, both western and eastern, that's long since disappeared forever. We're all the same now. Kind of.

ONE FOR THE ROAD

Back in the top flight in 1976/77, Johnny Giles took his team for a difficult away trip to Portman Road, Ipswich, where his Albion side found themselves on the end of a seven-goal mauling, with goals from Whymark, Mariner, Beattie and company flying in from everywhere. At the conclusion of the game, the team slowly dragged themselves back to the dressing room to incur the wrath, or so they thought, of manager Giles. Instead, Giles told them to put the game behind them, and joked with the shell-shocked keeper, John Osborne, nicknaming him 007! Back on the coach, Giles immediately ordered the coach driver to find the nearest off-licence and the remainder of the trip home was a blur for some of the team! Albion then went on a little run of success, with one defeat in nine games, the only defeat being at the hands of Manchester City 1-0, at Maine Road. Later, Osborne often joked that the next morning his wife called him to get out of bed. "John, it's gone eight!" He sat bolt upright in bed and shouted back; "Have they scored another?" Albion had the last laugh, putting four past the Ipswich defence without reply, in the return fixture, the following March, Laurie Cunningham's home debut for the Throstles.

ABANDON HOPE ALL YE WHO ENTER HERE

Down the years, only 24 games in Albion's history haven't made it through to the end once they've kicked off. From the weather to Warnock, here are the games that couldn't make it through:

10/02/1883 ....Albion 1 Notts Rangers 1........................... Friendly
Abandoned after 60 minutes.
12/11/1883 ....Stoke City 1 Albion 1............................... Friendly
Abandoned after 80 minutes.
03/12/1883 ....Albion 1 Cocknage 0...................Staffordshire Cup
Abandoned after 40 minutes but the result was allowed to stand. Albion went on to reach the final but lost to Mitchell St Georges, 4–0, at Wednesbury.
26/01/1884 ....Albion 2 Wednesbury Old Athletic 0 .... Friendly
Abandoned after 15 minutes due to a gale.
25/04/1885 ....Bolton Wanderers 1 Albion 0 .... Friendly
Abandoned after 70 minutes.
28/12/1885 ....Albion 0 Bolton Wanderers 0 .... Friendly
Abandoned after 75 minutes.
30/03/1889 ....Albion 4 Grimsby Town 0 .... Friendly
Abandoned after 60 minutes.
05/12/1892 ....Albion 1 Aston Villa 1................................ Friendly
Abandoned after 35 minutes.
09/03/1895 ....Stoke City 1 Albion 2.........................Division One
Abandoned after 68 minutes due to heavy rain. It was replayed on 25/03/1895 and ended in a 1–1 draw.
07/12/1895 ....Albion 0 Bury 0 ....Division One
Abandoned after 15 minutes because of heavy snow. It was replayed on 09/03/1896 and Albion were beaten 3–1.
18/11/1905 ....Grimsby Town 1 Albion 1 ....Division Two
Abandoned after 65 minutes owing to fog. It was replayed on 03/02/06, Grimsby winning 3–2.
19/01/1907 ....Albion 0 Barnsley 0 .... Division Two.
Abandoned after 80 minutes owing to fog. Replayed on 25/04/1907, Albion beating Barnsley 3–1.

06/01/1912......................Albion 0 Tottenham Hotspur 0.........Division One
Abandoned after 52 minutes because of bad light and fog. It was replayed on 13/03/1912, Albion winning 2-0.

13/02/1915.....................Oldham Athletic 0 Albion 1..............Division One
Abandoned after 21 minutes because of snow. It was replayed on 09/03/1915, ending in a 1-1 draw.

19/09/1925.....................Albion 0 Bury 2.................................Division One
Abandoned after 51 minutes because of heavy rain. The game was replayed on 09/11/1925, and Albion won 4-0, the sun shining upon the righteous.

22/02/1936.....................Albion 1 Aston Villa 0........................Division One
Abandoned after 26 minutes because of snow. It was played again on 01/03/1936 and Albion lost 3-0.

26/12/1944.....................Aston Villa 3 Albion 4....................Wartime fixture
Abandoned after 81 minutes because of fog. The result was allowed to stand, presumably to help morale on the home front.

9/11/1949.......................Albion 1 Blackpool 2..........................Division One
Abandoned after 70 minutes because of fog. It was replayed on 26/04/1950, Albion winning 1-0.

20/12/1958.....................Albion 1 Luton Town 1.......................Division One
Abandoned after 70 minutes because of heavy rain. Albion won the replayed game 2-0 on 15/04/1959.

26/12/1962.....................Wolverhampton W 2 Albion 0..........Division One
Abandoned after 45 minutes because of heavy snow. The match was replayed on 16/03/1963 and Albion lost 7-0, a typically shabby Wolverhampton trick.

14/12/1965.....................Albion 0 Aston Villa 0........................Division One
Abandoned after 51 minutes due to heavy rain. It was played again on 11/02 1966 and finished in a 2-2 draw.

16/05/1970.....................Lanerossi Vicenza 1 Albion 1 ... Anglo-Italian Cup
Abandoned after 76 minutes when the crowd, officials and players indulged in a spontaneous punch-up. The result was allowed to stand.

16/01/1973.....................Nottingham Forest 1 Albion 1.......................FAC3
This replay was abandoned after 79 minutes because of fog. The replayed replay ended in a 0-0 draw before Albion finally won 3-1 in a second replay at Filbert Street after 379 minutes of football.

16/03/2002.....................Sheffield United 0 Albion 3...............Division One
Abandoned after 82 minutes when Sheffield United were reduced to six players after two sendings off and an outbreak of falling over. The result was allowed to stand following an FA enquiry.

HOO-RAY

Raymond Christopher Patrick Treacy joined Albion as a youngster in 1961, a raw 15-year-old. The Irishman turned pro in 1964, and was capped by the Republic of Ireland before he had made his first-team debut for the Baggies. His Albion debut came against Sunderland at Roker Park in December 1966, Ray scoring in the 2-2 draw. In February 1968, with his first-team opportunities being limited, Ray opted to join Charlton Athletic. In August 1976, after his spell at Charlton and further spells at Preston North End and Oldham Athletic, Ray rejoined Albion under Johnny Giles. Ray then made his second debut for Albion against Derby County at the Baseball Ground, and once again featured in another 2-2 draw, scoring both Albion goals. In his two spells at The Hawthorns, Ray only managed 28 first-team appearances, notching seven goals.

COMMUNICATION BREAKDOWN

Some seek fame, others have fame thrust upon them. And some achieve infamy. He tried his best, he worked damned hard, he enjoyed success elsewhere. But as far as Albion supporters go, Bobby Gould is the manager whose name we prefer not to speak, a bit like Ron Saunders with eyebrows. Robert Anthony Gould had been at the Albion as a player, of course, enjoying a comparatively prolific 15 months in the early 1970s after he had been signed by Don Howe to partner Jeff Astle. That said, as an erstwhile worshipper from the dark side of Staffordshire, from where we signed him for £66,666 – and if that number wasn't an omen, what was? – Gould was always going to struggle to gain acceptance and before long, he was shuffling away to the West Country and a spell with Bristol City.

Gould returned to The Hawthorns with the Throstles approaching their lowest ebb, having just suffered the ignominy of a home thrashing from Woking in the FA Cup. From there, Brian Talbot was sacked, briefly replaced by Stuart Pearson before Bobby arrived to steer us unerringly towards relegation and the toga party at Twerton Park. We are all aware that the following campaign, 1991/92, was an unmitigated disaster, perhaps the worst ever endured given it was the first time the club had slumped as low as the third tier of English football and still weren't good enough to even qualify for the play-offs.

It was a bizarre season of fans being dragged into the dressing room, reporters being banned, coffins on the pitch, players sent out to apologise and some of the most awful, one dimensional drivel seen on any football field this side of Staffordshire. No, football doesn't always have to be pretty, but does it really need to look like a train derailment? Many of the stories are already the stuff of legend but one lesser known tale pretty much sums up a season of misadventure. The identity of the teller must remain a state secret, but it was told as the gospel truth. It took place in early season at Bolton's old Burnden Park ground. Gould had put a premium on set pieces in training, so much so that Albion had a dozen different routines, all of them individually numbered. Not the best idea in a game whose participants traditionally struggle to count up to one.

Prior to the Bolton game, the manager had berated the players for using the wrong option at the wrong time, insisting that if they'd only delivered the proper corner, all would have been sweetness and light. "At Bolton, when we get a corner, I'll tell you which number we're going to use." So, the game progressed and eventually, the Throstles won a corner over on the far side from the dugouts, and Tony Ford went to take it. "Hang on, which one does the gaffer want us to use?" went the cry from his colleagues. Unfortunately, there was something of a slope at Bolton, so much so that Ford couldn't see the manager on the opposite side of the field, frantically waving his fingers in the air like John McCririck having a seizure. So Ford stopped, and started to walk across the field in order to get a better view of his boss and be able to do what he was told. On his way, he was intercepted by the referee who gave him the shortest of shrift for wasting time, telling him to go and get on with the game.

In the meantime however, there'd been a brainwave on the Albion bench. These were in those far off days before fourth officials – whatever did we do without them? – when each club had numbered boards to indicate substitutions. So, to get the point across to Ford, the number three was held up. At which point Graham Harbey looked disgustedly at the bench and started to troop off the field, thinking he was about to be substituted. Harbey got near the halfway line without any of the Albion hierarchy having seen him coming, because they were all gesticulating wildly towards Ford, waving the number three in the air, desperately trying to attract his attention as he hastened back to the corner flag under instruction from the ref. Harbey arrived at the halfway line without a replacement substitute in sight, only to be greeted with, "What the hell are you doing here? Get back out there!" Only phrased rather more industrially. The referee was, by now, going purple at this perceived time wasting, and came across to order everyone on the Albion bench to sit down and roared at Tony Ford to get on with the game. Finally, two minutes of mayhem later, the wrong corner was taken. Bolton Wanderers 3 West Bromwich Albion 0. It was going to be a very, very long year.

THE GREAT ESCAPE

As of the 2009/10 campaign, there is still only one team in the 18-season history of the Premier League which has found itself bottom of the table on Christmas Day and yet still managed to climb to safety by season's end – the Albion. Survival looked a long way away as the Throstles slunk away from Birmingham City on the Saturday before Christmas after a 4-0 thrashing at the hands of Steve Bruce's team to leave them flat bottom, a situation worsened when Liverpool arrived at The Hawthorns to beat the Baggies 5-0 on Boxing Day. The turning point came when Albion, reduced to ten men early on after Thomas Gaardsoe collected a straight red card, managed to get a 1-1 draw at Manchester City without having a single shot on target, Richard Dunne confusing David James and putting through his own goal late on to give Albion a crucial point. From there, Albion kept themselves in the fight, particularly once the inspirational Kieran Richardson arrived on loan from Manchester United but, ahead of their penultimate game at Old Trafford, they knew they needed at least a point to have a chance of survival on the final day. They conceded a first-half goal from a Ryan Giggs free kick and immediately lost goalkeeper Russell Hoult to an injury, but the Pole in goal, Tomasz Kuszczak, came on and was inspired, keeping United at bay – and earning himself a move to United into the bargain – until a Robert Earnshaw spot kick won that crucial draw to set up the final-day drama against Portsmouth at The Hawthorns.

Albion kicked the day off on the bottom of the Premier League table. They kicked off the second half of the game still bottom of the table, but

with Southampton and Norwich City both losing, once Albion moved ahead against Pompey through goals from Geoff Horsfield and Kieran Richardson, it was a straight fight to the death with Crystal Palace. They were leading at Charlton Athletic with ten minutes to go, a result that would have doomed the Throstles. But Fortune favoured Bryan Robson and his team – Jonathan Fortune, who stepped up to equalise for the Addicks late in the day. Albion's game finished a couple of minutes earlier than Palace's, but finally, the result came through and the tension was over. Palace had drawn their London derby game, we were safe and Robson's team had created history.

THE FULL TWELVE YARDS

Only once in the history of the club have Albion's first and last goal of the season both been scored from the penalty spot. In the opening game of the 1996/97 season, the Baggies lost 2-1 at home to Barnsley, Andy Hunt scoring Albion's goal from the 12-yard mark. In the final game of that season, Albion also lost 2-1, this time at Stoke City on an historic afternoon which marked the final league game at the Victoria Ground. Andy Hunt was once again on the mark for the Baggies, netting from the spot. Our luck against Stoke hasn't improved any time since then either. Bookending the season with successful spot kicks would not have been possible in 1969/70 given that we were awarded just one penalty all season. On October 25th 1969, Tony Brown stepped up to take that spot kick against Manchester United at the Birmingham Road End of The Hawthorns. United were winning 1-0 at that stage, and England international Alex Stepney denied him with a fine save. Tony made up for that rare blemish by equalising in the second half and Bobby Hope then completed the turnaround by scoring Albion's winner, giving the Throstles a first home win of the season at the eighth attempt – they'd already won at Southampton, West Ham and Crystal Palace.

Getting a penalty to open our goalscoring account has been something of a rarity right throughout Albion history – it had only happened seven times to the end of the 2009/10 season. The first came in 1907/08 when Fred Buck scored from the spot against Wolverhampton Wanderers to set the Albion on the way to a 2-1 win. Buck made something of a habit of scoring Albion's first of the season from a penalty kick, for he did it again the following season

– against Grimsby Town in a 1-1 draw – and then once more in 1912/13 in a 2-0 win over Middlesbrough, the first time it had been done at The Hawthorns, the other two penalties coming on our travels. We had to wait until 1981/82 for the next occurrence, David Mills doing the job in a 2-1 defeat against Manchester City at Maine Road. Craig Shakespeare started the 6-3 Hawthorns rout of Exeter City from the spot in the 1991/92 campaign then Andy Hunt was next to do the job in 1996/97 against Barnsley. The most recent occurrence came in 2008/09 when Roman Bednar slotted in a penalty as Albion lost 2-1 at home to Everton.

FOR KING AND COUNTRY

After the outbreak of the Great War, football as we knew it ceased for the duration of the hostilities at the conclusion of the 1914/15 season, although that season itself was heavily disrupted as players were regularly called up for active service. Football would not return on a normal basis until 1919/20. As was the case throughout football – and society – many Albion players and officials found themselves involved in the conflict in some way, and a number served with distinction in foreign fields. It's thought that Sam Hatton was the first Albion man to join up, in November 1914, when he was conscripted into the South Staffordshire Territorials. Indeed, a company was raised within this battalion which consisted of Albion supporters. It was reported at the time that there was no shortage of volunteers, testimony to the courage of Black Countrymen. Sam was stationed in Ireland for a short time, became a sergeant and was decorated, receiving the Military Medal. Fred Morris joined the Royal Flying Corps as an air mechanic, and saw service in both France and Egypt. Alf Bentley became a lieutenant in the Leicestershire Regiment and was wounded in action in France. Other conscripts into the armed forces from the Albion 'clan' were Matt Wood (private in the Yorkshire Regiment), Luke Walters (corporal with RASC), Arthur Swift (corporal in the Lincolnshire Regiment), Alonzo Poulton (saw service with the South Staffordshire Regiment), and the club's assistant secretary, Ephraim Smith, who served as a lance corporal in the King's Own Scottish Borderers, seeing active service in France. Many others also served. Ben Shearman was a gunner at Aldershot, Hubert Pearson was also a gunner, and Fred Reed was a sergeant instructor with the Royal Fusiliers. Even at boardroom level, the Albion did their bit with Major H. Ely, a director, joining the RFA Battery. Another player, Jack Crisp, joined the Royal Navy as an electrical artificer with other Hawthorns personnel, reserve team keeper, Chris Crutchley joining the Royal Engineers, and Mr A. E. Lea seeing service as a sergeant, with the Royal Warwickshire Regiment. He also received the Military Medal. A total of 17 players, officials, and personnel, served in that terrible conflict. All of the aforementioned returned home to continue their normal lives but several made the ultimate sacrifice. Lieutenants Harold Bache and William Jackson were both killed in action, whilst former Albion junior, Billy Vale, lost his life in 1916. Following the war, a memorial tablet to these men was erected at The Hawthorns.

ACROSS THE GREAT DIVIDE

Born in Belfast, Northern Ireland in September 1919, Jack Vernon grew up in a community where Gaelic football dominated the sporting scene, and anyone who played soccer, as it was known in Ireland, was frowned upon – you only played one or the other with the general rule being that if you played in a soccer match, then you were automatically suspended from the Gaelic football association. Vernon was always a soccer man and when he joined Dundella in his native Belfast, the Gaelic Football Association barred him for life. He explained; "My 'crime' was to make up the numbers in a team. I turned out at inside-right for a junior club taking part in a summer league match. Unfortunately, I was spotted, and they read me the riot act." The GFA gave Jack a chance to redeem himself, but his mind was made up and his sporting path was well and truly chosen. Jack reflected; "That warning, in itself, would have been enough to make me play again out of sheer bravado. The truth was I liked football so I defied the authority, played soccer again, and was duly suspended." Jack joined Dundella, as an inside-right at first but reverted to centre-half, remaining there for the rest of his career. He was spotted by Belfast Celtic who he joined, and then signed for Albion from them, in November 1947, for £9,500, on a five-year contract. In his junior days prior to joining the Baggies, Jack played several times against the great Tommy Lawton, England's centre forward, who became Jeff Astle's mentor in later years. "I always managed to have a good game, and apparently impressed the officials who were looking on. Poor Tommy, he must have found every game extra strenuous with every unknown centre-half he met straining every nerve to stop him." With Albion, Jack went on to amass 200 first-

team appearances at the club, scoring one goal, a Christmas Day winner at Hillsborough against Sheffield Wednesday in 1948, during Albion's promotion season, when he led Albion back to the First Division. Vernon was capped 22 times for his country, 17 times as captain. He also skippered the United Kingdom side that played against Wales in 1951. At the end of his Albion career, Jack returned on a 'free' to his native Belfast to join Crusaders with whom he saw out his playing days, retiring in June 1954, to take over his family butchers business. Sadly, he passed away in 1981, at the early age of 62 years.

FORZA ALBION

Under head coach Roberto Di Matteo, Albion enjoyed a record-breaking promotion season in 2009/10. The Throstles amassed 91 points, eclipsing the 89 points gathered in the first promotion to the Premier League in 2001/02. Albion were particularly successful on their travels, losing only three games – 3-1 at Barnsley, 2-1 at Bristol City and 3-1 at Queens Park Rangers – equalling the record set in 1901/02 when the Baggies were Second Division champions in a 34-, rather than 46-game season. Albion's best performance in a 42-game season was just four away defeats in 1978/79 while in a 46-game campaign the six defeats in 2003/04 had previously been the best. In addition, the three away defeats was the best record in all four divisions in 2009/10, while the 41 goals Albion mustered was equalled only by Norwich City on their way to winning League One. Another peculiarity was that in every game following the turn of the year, Albion scored at least once. The closest they came to failing to hit the back of the net was on the final day of the season when it took until injury time for Graham Dorrans to score in the 1-1 draw at home to Barnsley, a goal which meant that no team managed to do the double over the Throstles in the course of the season, though manager Neil Warnock managed it – 1-0 at The Hawthorns with Crystal Palace, then 3-1 at Loftus Road.

COMINGS AND GOINGS

Whether the club's foundation date be 1878 or 1879, according to which historian you give the most credence, West Bromwich Albion has been around a good long while now. And in each of those years there have been births and deaths of those who have played their part in Albion history, so we present for you an addition to, and subtraction from, the Albion story from throughout the club's history.

Year	Born	Died
1879	John Knowles	
1880	Fred Buck	
1881	George Dorsett	
1882	James Bowden	
1883	Jesse Pennington	
1884	George Elmore	
1885	Sam Edwards	
1886	Hubert Pearson	
1887	Alf Bentley	
1888	Len Moorwood	
1889	H. G. Bache	
1890	Arthur Cook	
1891	Sid Bowser	Albert Aldridge
1892	William Adams	
1893	Fred Morris	
1894	Bobby Blood	
1895	Clifford Sambrooke	
1896	John Crisp	
1897	John Byers	
1898	George Ashmore	
1899	Joe Carter	
1900	James Spencer	Harry Green
1901		William Hendry
1902	Tommy Glidden	
1903	Horace Smith	Luther Walker
1904	Jimmy Cookson	
1905	Jimmy Edwards	
1906	Joe Evans	
1907		James Millar
1908	Harold Pearson	
1909	W. G. Richardson	
1910	Teddy Sandford	Ted Pheasant
1911	Cecil Shaw	
1912	Jack Sankey	Samuel Nicholls

1913	Geoff Spencer	Arthur Randall
1914	James Prew	Jimmy McLean
1915	George Tranter	
1916	James Pemberton	H. G. Bache
1917	James Southam	John Swallow
1918	William Tudor	Tom Pearson
1919	Len Millard	
1920	Jack Haines	
1921	Arthur Smith	Thomas Green
1922	Ernest Robinson	George Holden
1923	Charles Evans	Henry Burton
1924	Dennis Gordon	George Wheldon
1925	Joe Kennedy	James Stevenson
1926	Ray Barlow	George Garratt
1927	Robert Barker	Alf Geddes
1928	Frank Griffin	John Paddock
1929	Ronnie Allen	Bob Roberts
1930	Derek Hogg	Arthur Cook
1931	Johnnie Nicholls	Roderick McLeod
1932	Jimmy Dugdale	Abraham Law
1933	Wilf Carter	Jem Bayliss
1934	Andrew Aitken	Harry Brown
1935	Derek Kevan	Henry Boyd
1936	Ray Crawford	Walter Jack
1937	Alec Jackson	Billy Bassett
1938	Stan Jones	Henry Aston
1939	Bobby Cram	John Crisp
1940	Clive Clark	Alf Bentley
1941	Doug Fraser	Amos Adams
1942	Jeff Astle	Henry Hadley
1943	Bobby Hope	George Dorsett
1944	Jim Cumbes	William Folks
1945	Tony Brown	Seth Powell
1946	Willie Johnston	John Manners
1947	Ian Collard	Harry Parkes
1948	David Shaw	Harry Bell
1949	Garry Pendrey	Henry Chambers
1950	David Cross	A. C. Jephcott

1951	Len Cantello	John Nevin
1952	Peter Latchford	Fred Buck
1953	Brendon Batson	Arthur Smith
1954	Gerry Armstrong	Joe Reader
1955	Tony Godden	Hubert Pearson
1956	Laurie Cunningham	Bobby McNeal
1957	Bryan Robson	Harry Jones
1958	Cyrille Regis	William Harper
1959	Tony Ford	W. G. Richardson
1960	Gary Bannister	Walter Boyes
1961	Martyn Bennett	Sid Bowser
1962	Gary Hackett	Fred Morris
1963	Paul Edwards	Edward Burton
1964	Graham Harbey	Jonathan Blagden
1965	Paul Agnew	Harold Dicken
1966	Don Goodman	Albert Evans
1967	Ian Hamilton	Fred Reed
1968	Richard Sneekes	Len Darnell
1969	Paul Mardon	Stan Butler
1970	Igor Balis	Jesse Pennington
1971	Jordao	Joe Evans
1972	Lee Ashcroft	Stan Davies
1973	Phil Gilchrist	George Ashmore
1974	Darren Moore	Tommy Glidden
1975	Michael Appleton	Sammy Heaselgrave
1976	Lee Hughes	Arthur Gale
1977	Kevin Kilbane	Joe Carter
1978	Neil Clement	William Arch
1979	Zoltan Gera	George Bytheway
1980	Adam & James Chambers	Arthur Davies
1981	Robert Earnshaw	Billy Gripton
1982	Lloyd Dyer	James Duggan
1983	Jonas Olsson	Norman Heath
1984	Chris Brunt	Arthur Fitton
1985	Scott Carson	William Richardson
1986	James Morrison	Joe Kennedy
1987	Graham Dorrans	Jack Haines
1988	Reuben Reid	Bobby Blood

1989	Marcus Haber	Laurie Cunningham
1990	Joe Mattock	Edward Connolly
1991	Chris Wood	George Lee
1992	Ryan Allsop	Gilbert Alsop
1993	George Thorne	Billy Light
1994		Harold Pearson
1995		Ted Sandford
1996		Jock Wallace
1997		Len Millard
1998		Dick Sheppard
1999		George Corbett
2000		Bob Finch
2001		Ronnie Allen
2002		Jeff Astle
2003		Jim Sanders
2004		Glyn Hood
2005		Stan Steele
2006		Jimmy Dudley
2007		Frank Griffin
2008		Jimmy Dugdale
2009		Sir Bobby Robson
2010		David Burnside

BY GEORGES

A man of many masks was Georges Santos, not least the protective one that he had to wear after he and Andy Johnson had something of a coming together on the field during a Tranmere versus Nottingham Forest game, Johnson's stray arm fracturing Georges' eye socket in an accidental collision which apparently upset Georges more than somewhat. Of this, more later. But the masks to which we refer are of the metaphorical kind, those of hero and of villain as far as his relationship with the Throstles is concerned. And it all started so well too, when the imposing Frenchman made his rendezvous with Monsieur Megson on transfer deadline day in 2000. Georges was one of the famous five firemen, come to Sandwell to put out the blazing wreck that was Albion's 1999/2000 season. You remember the one, a bit like the *Towering Inferno* only more incendiary and without so much hope. And then Steve McQueen came riding over the hill on his bike – OK, we're mixing films, but you get the drift – in the shape of Gary Megson. Megson came hurtling towards the disaster with buckets of water in tow, Frank Burrows behind him, busily trying to pump up the water pressure and get the hoses working while also trying to fan the flames out with his flat cap. Leaping from the fire engine ready to help put out the blaze were Neil Clement, Desmond Lyttle, Tony Butler, Bob Taylor and Santos, a mixture of permanent signings and loan moves, all designed to bolster a flagging squad and to help keep the Baggies from taking the unthinkable drop back into the third tier, a drop that was coming closer by the day. Santos signed for the Albion on a short-term deal until the end of the season, £25,000 going to Tranmere Rovers in return for his services, and it turned out to be money well spent. Santos stepped straight into the midfield and began shoring things up from the outset, giving us a little more defensive insurance to allow the likes of Richard Sneekes to do their work further upfield. Albion collected a very hard-won ten points from those last eight games, nothing special perhaps, but just enough to unleash scenes of rapture on the final afternoon of the season when we defeated Charlton Athletic to remain in Division One.

That, we thought, was that, for Georges left The Hawthons in the summer, going to Sheffield United and the chance to work with Neil Warnock following the end of his Albion deal. Just another footnote in the silk stocking of history, a player who had done his bit and would barely trouble our minds again. Then, on March 16th 2002, Albion headed north for a game at Bramall Lane. A tricky fixture and one that we needed to win if we were going to keep the pressure on Wolves in the hunt for automatic promotion. It was a trip to Yorkshire that started beautifully, United's goalkeeper getting himself sent off for handball outside the area just nine minutes in, Scott Dobie giving Albion the lead nine minutes later. Albion were in cruise control, Derek McInnes unleashing the goal of the season, a screamer from the edge of the box after being picked out by an Igor Balis corner, the Throstles utterly untroubled by the opposition as they passed the hour mark and Neil Warnock made a double substitution, bringing on Santos and Patrick Suffo in the 64th minute.

Did I mention that by this time, Andy Johnson, serial eye socket interferer, had joined the Albion? I didn't? Well, he had, and this was the first time he and the somewhat aggrieved Santos had shared a football pitch since that moment. It's at times like this that you find out who your friends are. Forty seconds after Santos came on, Derek McInnes rolled a pass towards Johnson, a pass that probably needed a bit more weight, a hospital ball of a pass, almost literally. Let's not suggest, not for one second, that Georges' lunge towards Jonno was premeditated, let's insist instead that Jonno was simply so swift in getting to the ball that Santos was late in the tackle. Johnson flew so high in the air after Santos had made contact with him that he came down carpeted in a light dusting of snow, following which he tried to get up and have a quiet word with Santos, only to find his teammates holding him down as the referee dismissed Santos after barely a minute on the pitch. Meanwhile in the ensuing confusion, Patrick Suffo headbutted McInnes, perhaps as retribution for the underhit pass that had started things off, but more likely because he was the only Albion player who was his height, and was also swiftly reminded where the dressing room was by referee Wolstenholme. To cap a wonderful afternoon, the Throstles finally completed a 3-0 win over Mr Warnock's team, even though the game finished seven minutes early.

I'M PART OF THE UNION

Albion's Former Players' Association has become well established in the last few years under the direction and guidance of the likes of Brendon Batson, Ray Wilson, Alistair Robertson and Geoff Snape. It's actually a rebirth of a concept that has roots that date back to the start of the 20th century. The original grouping came into being when, at the Roebuck Hotel, New Street, a meeting was held in February 1902 to inaugurate an Old Players' Union, those in attendance including George Woodhall, Arthur Loach, Dennis Smith, Arthur Biddulph, George Timmins, Jack Horton, James Stanton, Harry Bell and George Bell. The Union was brought into being in order to offer 'pecuniary assistance' to any former player in need of help, and it was proposed that a benefit game be held annually to raise funds.

Inside 18 months, they had dispensed some £300, leaving the coffers empty even though "they still have the orphan children of the late W. Bisseker and Luther Walker to look after, and an appeal has been made to them on behalf of George Cave who has been ill over two years and for some months has had to pay £3 3s. a week to support him in a sanatorium". Exact details on how and why the Players' Union was disbanded are hard to find, but it's believed that it folded following the outbreak of the Great War when efforts to raise money for the war effort and its victims superseded pretty much all other charities.

BACK IN THE USSR

For West Bromwich Albion, 'Glasnost' came over 50 years ago, in early 1957, when on April 26th, secretary Ephraim Smith received an invitation from the Football Association to undertake an arduous, ground-breaking tour of the USSR, essentially a forerunner of the more celebrated jaunt to the People's Republic of China made by Ron Atknson's side in May 1978. The Soviet tour would be of 16 days' duration, with three matches against Zenit Leningrad, Dynamo Tbilisi and CDSA, otherwise known as the 'Red Army'. It was the equivalent of playing Juventus, AC Milan and Internazionale, only with tanks.

One major problem foreseen by Smith was that as the tour was scheduled to commence on May 29th, it would mean the players returning early from their summer break, after being out of training for a month since the end of the season. As the *Albion News* reflected in its tour report early the following season, these problems were overcome by the players' willingness to undertake such a historic commitment. So it was that the tour party of 23, resplendent in new suits commissioned for the occasion, gathered at Snow Hill Station, Birmingham at 9 am on May 29th. Included in the party were the chairman, Major H. Wilson-Keys, directors Jim Gaunt and Sid Sheppard, manager Vic Buckingham, trainer Dick Graham and players Ray Barlow, Ronnie Allen, Fred Brown, Jimmy Dudley, Frank Griffin, Roy Horobin, Don Howe, Joe Kennedy, Gordon Lee, Len Millard, Bobby Robson, Jim Sanders, Maurice Setters, Brian Whitehouse and Stuart Williams. They were joined by Eric Woodward, the very popular correspondent with the *Birmingham Post*, while another noted pressman, Charles Harrold, of the *News Chronicle*, was to join up at London Heathrow Airport. A notable absentee from the group was Derek Kevan, part of the touring England 'B' side to Bulgaria, Romania and Czechoslovakia. The Tank would roll in when the party were en route to Russia. In a later *Football Monthly* interview, Kevan spoke of that summer in which he covered around 9,000 miles for club and country. Kevan also revealed, somewhat sheepishly, that he actually joined the Albion party two days later than scheduled, having forgotten his visa in Prague.

The outward journey to the Soviet Union was like nothing any of the players had experienced before. They travelled via Copenhagen and Stockholm, leaving a hot and sticky Heathrow Airport at 5 pm on May 29th, to arrive at a rather colder Riga Airport, Moscow, at 5 pm the following day. Following a very pleasant and lavish reception in Moscow, the squad then had to endure a ten-hour train journey, overnight, to Leningrad, where their first match against Zenit was to be played. This, the *Albion News* was to report, was very traumatic to say the least, and the report's anonymous author, probably Eph Smith, noted; "Either the track was faulty, or the axles were worn, and there was very little sleep for anyone in the party who were mightily relieved to see daylight." However, the group arrived safely in Leningrad, in fine fettle for their contest against Zenit, which was to be played in the Kirov Stadium, in front of a capacity deeply partisan crowd of 80,000. Reporting on that match, Charles Harrold assessed the Zenit side as being 'good on the ball' and probably on a par with a side in the lower half of our First Division. He also hailed the fact that the 'man of the match' was Albion's number six, the great Ray Barlow, who seemingly everyone had heard of, and Barlow was; "Heartily cheered by all of the assembled 80,000 gathered to witness this great occasion." Which is precisely as it should be in the presence of greatness, though if they were doing things properly, they'd have knocked up a statue in his honour and renamed the city Barlowgrad.

Albion's other hero that day was undoubtedly Derek Kevan. Having only arrived a few hours before the kick-off, due to his previously described exertions with the England 'B' team, he appeared as a second-half substitute, for the unlucky Roy Horobin, who, Harrold reported, "Was not injured", and Kevan promptly scored a brilliant goal to put Albion into the lead. As most of the second half was played in driving rain, good old English conditions that The Tank would enjoy, it was hardly surprising that he was in his element but, unfortunately, the Throstles could not hold onto the advantage, and Goolevski equalised for the hosts to ensure that honours were even at the final whistle. A fair result, as Harrold again reflected, and "A great day for Albion". Albion's line-up that day was: Brown, Howe, Millard, Setters, Kennedy, Barlow (captain), Griffin, Robson, Horobin, Allen and Lee. Kevan replaced Roy Horobin at half-time. All of the officials were non-Russian, such was the emphasis that the hosts put on this match as an 'international' fixture.

By now, Albion were big news wherever they went, and were feted by frenzied football fans and press alike. For the second fixture of the tour, against Dynamo Tbilisi on June 7th, the party had to be split into two travelling groups, with a five-hour gap, in order for the latter group to conduct a goodwill visit to the Imperial Summer Palace of the Tsars. The *Albion News* recorded; "This group spent the morning talking to groups of Russian people, including young boys. The conversation being entirely possible as English is taught as a 'compulsory' language in all Russian schools." This kind of planned activity also gave an indication of the importance the hosts attributed to this tour. The Russian public also turned out in numbers with an estimated two to three thousand fans turning up to watch Albion's training sessions prior to their second fixture at the Dynamo Stadium. Albion lined up with three changes from the Zenit fixture: Jim Sanders replaced Fred Brown in goal, Stuart Williams came in at left-back for Len Millard and Derek Kevan came into the side in place of Gordon Lee, with Horobin switching to the left wing and Ronnie Allen reverting to his customary role at centre forward. Half-time substitutes for the Baggies were Jimmy Dudley for Maurice Setters and Brian Whitehouse for Bobby Robson.

The match was played on an intensely hot day, but the pre-match reception was equally warm, described as 'incredible' by the *Albion News*. The 35,000-capacity crowd witnessed the Albion players being presented with huge bouquets of local flowers and fruits from the region, displayed with images of small birds, which would appear to have been the hosts' attempts to create the Throstle image which, it was reported, had; "Intrigued them so very much." Albion went into this fixture full of confidence and it is important to note that Dynamo Tbilisi were in fact top of the Russian national league and considered one of the strongest sides in the Soviet Union. The fact that Albion were about to brush them aside 3-0 to become the first English side to defeat a Russian side in Russia shows the enormity of the result. From the kick-off, Albion made good use of the 'long ball' game, which totally confused their opponents. Barlow, Kennedy and Stuart Williams were described as 'imperious' in defence while up front, Allen and Kevan caused the hosts' rearguard all sorts of problems. The crowd, it was reported, enjoyed Kevan's bustling style, and Ronnie Allen's 'wanderings'. Roy Horobin, having one of his best games for Albion, scored the first goal after 16 minutes and Kevan increased the lead just before the break. Just after the interval, Kevan added a third and it was game over, 3-0 at the final whistle, and a rather 'humbling' reflection from the *Albion News* stating: "The Albion side were cheered from the pitch by the Russian crowd, it was one of the most wonderful experiences we have ever enjoyed." Tribute indeed! Fans also gathered in their thousands at the post-match reception to once again show their appreciation of their English visitors.

The final match of the tour was against the Red Army side in Moscow on June 12th. This game was played in the magnificent Lenin Stadium, which had a capacity of 103,000. The *Albion News* reporter enthusiastically told his readers: "This magnificent arena has a bewildering 1,000 rooms, including 6 large dressing rooms and 30 smaller dressing rooms. No fewer than 14 gymnasiums, 40 buffet bars for spectators, each with its own refrigerator, two cinema halls, an orchestra studio, and if that wasn't enough, an in-built hotel comprising 100 rooms for competitors. Press facilities, given this was 50 years ago, were also magnificent, boasting an impressive in-built Telegraph Office and Post Office, with outside links to 26 countries. This impressive structure was completed in July 1956, and took all of one year to build."

Albion went into this game with two main changes Fred Brown returned in place of Jim Sanders and Brian Whitehouse replaced Bobby Robson. Unfortunately, during the game skipper Ray Barlow became unwell and was replaced by Jimmy Dudley. One other change; Bobby Robson replaced Brian Whitehouse at half-time. The Baggies started brightly enough, but were quickly on the back foot when Maurice Setters unluckily put through his own goal after 15 minutes. Within five minutes, Albion were level when Whitehouse headed home a Ronnie Allen cross. On 32 minutes Albion took the lead with the goal of the game. Derek Kevan picked up a Don Howe pass on the halfway line. Kevan then ploughed his way through the Russian rearguard brushing off two or three defenders to score a truly memorable goal. Three minutes later, a great interchange between Kevan and Whitehouse resulted in the latter adding Albion's third. Unfortunately, Albion went to sleep within minutes and Rishkov reduced the arrears to go into the break 3-2 down. Kevan added a fourth early in the second half, and from that point the result was never in doubt. So a truly memorable tour came to an end, and to come through it unbeaten against strong Russian opposition was impressive. Of course, this was not to be the end of the story. On October 29th that year, the Red Army repaid the compliment and came to play Albion at a packed Hawthorns. A crowd of 52,805 were in the ground that night and witnessed an eleven-goal spectacular, with an imperious Albion swamping their Russian opponents 6-5. Hardly swamped you might say, but when Desmond Hackett's account of the match was published, it read '6-5 But West Brom Walk It'. Hackett concluded that only for 30 minutes were the Russians really a threat, before being 'swept aside by magnificent Albion'. The crowd thrilled to the performance of the 'England class' Derek Kevan. Despite being pushed, pulled and hauled down by the opposition defenders throughout the match, he was superb all night and helped himself to two late goals. For the record, Don Howe scored Albion's first goal, equalising Busonov's earlier effort on 17 minutes. Bobby Robson put the Baggies ahead for the first time before being pegged back within a minute by a Bubukin equaliser. Frank Griffin put Albion ahead again, just before the break, to complete a three-goals-in-five-minutes spell. Ronnie Allen increased Albion's lead from the penalty spot just after the break, when the 'awesome Kevan' was pulled down. Incidentally, the same scenario resulted in Allen blasting another 'spot-kick' wide of the post, which, Hackett reflected, was 'a just outcome' as the referee's decision he thought to be 'somewhat harsh'. Busonov reduced the arrears to 4-3 on 66 minutes, before Kevan put the game beyond doubt with two goals after 70 and 77 minutes. Still time for a late Russian rally, with goals from the ever-dangerous Busonov, and another from Emishev. Final score: Albion 6 Red Army 5. Now that's entertainment!

HARDAKER'S FOLLY

The Football League Cup was introduced for the 1960/61 season but it was anything but an overnight success as many clubs, including Albion, refused to enter. Alan Hardaker, secretary of the Football League, was one of the competition's prime movers along with Stanley Rous, in order to exploit the sudden expansion of and enthusiasm for floodlit midweek football. Albion's entry into the competition in 1965/66 paved the way for the first-ever senior meeting with Walsall in round two, Albion having a bye from the first round. Tony Brown netted the club's first goal in the competition in the 3-1 win. Bomber scored in every round that season

– ten in nine games – including scoring in the home leg of the two-legged final when West Ham United were beaten 5-3 on aggregate to win the competition at the first time of asking. Clive Clark matched Bomber's feat the following season, outdoing Brown by scoring not just in every game, but every match, including the final when he became the first player ever to score in a League Cup final at Wembley. He finished on the losing side as the Baggies lost 3-2 to his former club, QPR.

That defeat to a Third Division side started a run of embarrassments in the competition as the Baggies were beaten 3-1 by Reading of the same division the following season, new boss Alan Ashman later saying it was the worst display of his time with Albion. In 1968/69, Albion were beaten 2-1 by Peterborough United at London Road in the second round to complete a hat-trick of calamities. Even so, the Throstles continued to excel in front of goal and scored in each of their first 23 League Cup ties, a sequence ended on October 29th 1969 when they drew 0-0 in the fifth round at Leicester City's Filbert Street. They won the replay 2-1 and went on to a third League Cup final in five seasons, losing to Manchester City at Wembley. The following season the Baggies lost 5-0 at Tottenham in the fourth round and were then beaten again by Spurs in their next League Cup tie the following season, the 1-0 defeat the first defeat in the League Cup at The Hawthorns after an unbeaten run of 13 games. That is the only time that Albion have lost to the same side on consecutive occasions, in League Cup campaigns, though Derby County beat the Throstles in both legs of the second round tie in 1986/87, Albion losing 5-1 on aggregate, the only goal scored by Steve Bull. That 5-0 beating from Spurs was the club's biggest defeat in the competition though they subsequently lost 6-1 at Nottingham Forest in the first leg of the second round on October 6th 1982. Albion won the largely academic second leg 3-1.

Fortunately, they only had to play Forest twice. On three occasions Albion have played the same opposition three times in a League Cup campaign. In 1978/79, they drew 0-0 with Leeds United at The Hawthorns in round two, came up goalless at Elland Road in the replay, then lost 1-0 in the second replay at Maine Road. In 1980/81 the Baggies drew 0-0 against Preston North End at The Hawthorns in round four, then drew 1-1 at Deepdale. They returned to The Hawthorns for replay two and the Throstles won 2-1. Finally, West Ham came up three times in 1981/82 over the course of round three, drawing 2-2 at Upton Park and then 1-1 back in God's country. Back to east London it was, the Throstles beating the Hammers 1-0.

IT'S DEJA VU ALL OVER AGAIN

In 1945/46, the first post-war season FA Cup games were two-legged affairs to guarantee each club at least one home game in a campaign where normal league football had yet to return. Albion met Derby County in the fourth round and lost both games, the only time they've ever lost twice in the cup in the same season. Derby won the cup for the first and, so far, only time that season. However, Albion have lost two cup ties in the same year on two occasions. In 1993, they were beaten on January 2nd by West Ham United in the third round, then lost to Halifax Town in the first round of the following season's competition on November 14th. In 1999, they were beaten 1-0 at AFC Bournemouth on January 2nd in round three, then were beaten by Blackburn Rovers, also in round three, on December 22nd. In 1968/69, Albion were beaten in the semi-final by Leicester City, 1-0 at Hillsborough. The third-round tie in 1969/70 saw the Throstles back at Hillsborough, losing 2-1 to Sheffield Wednesday, the only time Albion have lost consecutive FA Cup ties at the same ground – they've never lost consecutive FA Cup ties at The Hawthorns.

HALFWAY THERE

Football cliché will tell you that nobody remembers the semi-finalists in any competition, but it's our duty to give the conventional wisdom a good kicking and lay before you the many occasions, and many competitions, in which the Throstles have stood on the threshold of the final. Only the result of the decisive game has been included – earlier drawn games leading to replays have been omitted.

25/03/1882	Birmingham Senior Cup	Wednesbury Old Athletic	2-3
24/02/1883	Wednesbury Cup	Aston Unity	1-0
10/03/1883	Staffordshire Senior Cup	Leek Whites	8-1
10/03/1884	Birmingham Cup	Walsall Town Swifts	0-1
28/02/1885	Staffordshire Cup	Walsall Town Swifts	0-2
06/03/1886	FA Cup	Small Heath	4-0
17/04/1886	Staffordshire Cup	Burton Wanderers	3-0

05/03/1887	FA Cup	Preston North End	3-1
24/03/1887	Staffordshire Cup	Wolverhampton Wanderers	3-1
08/02/1888	FA Cup	Derby Junction	3-0
11/02/1888	Birmingham Cup	Wolverhampton Wanderers	2-0
17/03/1888	Staffordshire Cup	Stoke City	1-0
16/03/1889	FA Cup	Preston North End	0-1
06/04/1889	Staffordshire Cup	Walsall Town Swifts	5-0
05/04/1890	Birmingham Cup	Walsall Town Swifts	2-1
12/04/1890	Staffordshire Cup	Walsall Town Swifts	2-3
28/02/1891	FA Cup	Blackburn Rovers	2-3
22/04/1891	Birmingham Cup	Aston Villa	2-3
19/03/1892	FA Cup	Nottingham Forest	6-2
09/04/1892	Birmingham Cup	Aston Villa	2-0
17/03/1894	Birmingham Cup	Loughborough	6-1
11/04/1894	Bass Charity Cup	Aston Villa	2-5
16/03/1895	FA Cup	Sheffield Wednesday	2-0
18/03/1895	Birmingham Cup	Small Heath	3-2
20/02/1897	Birmingham Cup	Wolverhampton Wanderers	0-3
20/09/1897	Birmingham Charity Cup	Aston Villa	0-3
22/01/1898	Staffordshire Cup	Small Heath	1-0
26/09/1898	Mayor of Birm. Cup	Walsall Town Swifts	1-3
16/10/1899	Mayor of Birm.Cup	Aston Villa	2-1
20/11/1899	Staffordshire Cup	Wolverhampton Wanderers	3-1
17/09/1900	Mayor of Birm. Cup	Walsall	6-1
08/04/1901	FA Cup	Tottenham Hotspur	0-4
07/10/1901	Staffordshire Cup	Small Heath	2-1
13/10/1902	Birmingham Cup	Walsall	7-1
27/10/1902	Staffordshire Cup	Wolverhampton Wanderers	4-0
21/09/1903	Mayor of Birm. Cup	Small Heath	4-5
22/10/1904	Birmingham Senior Cup	Burslem Port Vale	2-1
18/09/1905	Mayor of Birm. Cup	Birmingham	2-1
23/03/1907	FA Cup	Everton	1-2
03/04/1912	FA Cup	Blackburn Rovers	1-0
14/03/1931	FA Cup	Everton	1-0
20/03/1935	FA Cup	Bolton Wanderers	2-0
08/04/1937	FA Cup	Preston North End	1-4
09/05/1942	League War Cup 1st leg	Wolverhampton Wanderers	0-4
16/05/1942	League War Cup 2nd leg	Wolverhampton Wanderers	0-3

15/04/1944...	Midland War Cup 1st leg...	Stoke City	1-1
22/04/1944...	Midland War Cup 2nd leg.	Stoke City	3-1
27/03/1954...	FA Cup	Port Vale	2-1
28/03/1957...	FA Cup	Aston Villa	0-1
01/12/1965...	League Cup 1st leg	Peterborough United	2-1
15/12/1965...	League Cup 2nd leg	Peterborough United	4-2
18/01/1967...	League Cup 1st leg	West Ham United	4-0
08/02/1967...	League Cup 2nd leg	West Ham United	2-2
27/04/1968...	FA Cup	Birmingham City	2-0
29/03/1969...	FA Cup	Leicester City	0-1
19/11/1969...	League Cup 1st leg	Carlisle United	0-1
03/12/1969...	League Cup 2nd leg	Carlisle United	4-1
04/08/1971...	Watney Cup	Halifax Town	2-0
08/04/1978...	FA Cup	Ipswich Town	1-3
03/02/1982...	League Cup 1st leg	Tottenham Hotspur	0-0
10/02/1982...	League Cup 2nd leg	Tottenham Hotspur	0-1
03/04/1982...	FA Cup	Queens Park Rangers	0-1
16/05/1993...	D2 Play-off 1st leg	Swansea City	1-2
19/05/1993...	D2 Play-off 2nd leg	Swansea City	2-0
13/05/2001...	D1 Play-off 1st leg	Bolton Wanderers	2-2
17/05/2001...	D1 Play-off 2nd leg	Bolton Wanderers	3-0
13/05/2007...	FLC Play-off 1st leg	Wolverhampton Wanderers	3-2
16/05/2007...	FLC Play-off 2nd leg	Wolverhampton Wanderers	1-0
05/04/2008...	FA Cup	Portsmouth	0-1

THE RED MENACE

Ahead of their return to the Premier League in 2010/11, the Throstles must have been dreading the coming encounters with one team in particular. Not only had Albion never even scored a Premier League goal against the Reds, their sequence of 11 straight defeats against them is the worst run of results against any team in the club's history. It all began inauspiciously enough in March 1985 when Liverpool came to The Hawthorns and won 5-0 in a First Division fixture – the Baggies had got a 0-0 up at Anfield the previous October, the club's most recent point against them. The following season Albion were thumped 4-1 on Merseyside, Garth Crooks scoring our last goal at Anfield, then as the Throstles hurtled towards relegation and near oblivion, Craig Madden got the consolation goal in a 2-1 Hawthorns defeat on April 21st 1986. Albion haven't put the ball in the Liverpool net since. The 2002/03 season saw Albion lose 2-0 at Liverpool, then surrender 6-0 at The Hawthorns, the club's worst home league defeat. When Albion returned to the top flight two years later, at least Liverpool had the good grace to stop at five when they won in the Black Country on Boxing Day, adding to a 3-0 Anfield win in September. Things improved a little as Albion were relegated again the following season losing 1-0 at Anfield on New Year's Eve, then 2-0 in West Bromwich. And in 2008/09, a 3-0 beating at Anfield was compounded by a 2-0 reverse at The Hawthorns in the 37th game of the campaign, a defeat that relegated the Throstles.

OIL CRISIS

The Albion career of John Hartson is not one that will go down as glorious in the annals of the club's history. Leaving Celtic for The Hawthorns was perhaps a move too many for the Welsh international who was clearly coming towards the end of what had been, up to then, a very successful goalscoring career. Of course, shortly after leaving The Hawthorns, the big man had to fight a rather more important battle, against cancer, one which had many of us fearing for his very life. The fact that he came through it all is testimony to his determination and self belief and everyone at the Albion was thrilled when he received the all clear.

Hartson's off the field demeanour belied the aggressive, in your face, centre forward that we were used to seeing. Instead he was a likeable, engaging figure, full of stories about the game and always willing to do his share of the media chores. An honourable man who paid his dues, the big Welsh striker was also a little on the forgetful side. On the day he signed for the Throstles he came to The Hawthorns to conduct the usual press conference duties, even going so far as to parade an Albion scarf and ball, as is tradition. His work for the day done, he jumped into his car to head back up to Glasgow in order to sort out his affairs at that end of the country prior to moving to the Midlands. Sensibly, before hitting the motorway, he filled up his car with petrol at the BP on the Birmingham Road. Walking to the counter to pay, John realised that he'd travelled without his wallet and had nothing to pay with. Fortunately, at the counter next to him, was the legendary siren of the commercial department, Sue Dabbs, sporting her Albion pass around her neck. Seizing upon the fact that they were fellow employees, albeit that John probably earned more in a week than Sue managed in a couple of years, he turned to her and said; "Hello. I'm John Hartson, I work at the Albion as well. You couldn't lend me thirty quid to pay for the petrol could you?" Reaching deep into her purse, Sue came up with the money and catastrophic "Striker steals petrol" headlines had been averted. Thanks to such heroic interventions, we in the media can continue to sleep soundly at our desks.

DOING TIME

Beyond the confines of the very biggest clubs, it's rare nowadays to find players who stay with one club over the bulk of their career, the majority staying for two or three seasons before heading off on a lucrative Bosman move. Understandable perhaps, but that loss of loyalty and the long-serving player has robbed football of a little of its identity, giving supporters fewer players with whom they can identify over a long period. Albion have been blessed with many loyal servants, the top ten of whom are listed, from the time the player signed professional for the club, to the time he left, was transferred or retired.

Hubert Pearson	20 years, 2 months	March 1906-May 1926
Jesse Pennington	19 years, 2 months	March 1903-May 1922
Tony Brown	18 years	October 1963-October 1981
Graham Williams	17 years	April 1955-April 1972
Alistair Robertson	17 years	September 1969-September 1986
W. G. Richardson	16 years, 5 months	June 1929-November 1945
Joe Smith	16 years	May 1910-May 1926
Len Millard	15 years, 9 months	September 1942-June 1958
Joe Reader	15 years, 8 months	August 1885-April 1901
Tommy Magee	15 years, 4 months	January 1919-May 1934

Tony Brown actually joined Albion as an amateur in April 1961, spending two years and six months on the groundstaff, before being signed as a professional by Jimmy Hagan. He continues his association with the club to this day, both as a regular columnist in the matchday programme and as an expert summariser with local radio. While Graham Williams joined the groundstaff at Albion as an amateur in September 1954, Alistair Robertson joined the groundstaff as an amateur in July 1968. Len Millard actually joined the club as an amateur before World War II, in May 1937, and made

his Baggies first-team debut at Northampton Town in August 1942, a
month before turning professional. Joe Reader joined Albion as an amateur
in January 1885, eight months before turning pro.

DRURY LANE

Footballers are not always the greatest of timekeepers, particularly when
it comes to getting in for training on time day after day. Chuck Drury, in
particular, seemed to find it difficult to make it to Albion's Spring Road
training ground on time, especially when, in his early days, he had to get
there by bus. Coming up with excuses to satisfy the management on such
a regular basis would tax anybody, but Drury was nothing if not ingenious,
perhaps his best excuse being that as he boarded the bus, a gust of wind blew
his hat off and he had to jump off the bus to retrieve it, making him late as
a consequence. Getting a car did little for Drury's punctuality, particularly
in the harsh winter of 1963. One morning, he was confronted with a four
feet wall of snow that was blocking his garage doors. Drury insisted that he
had no shovel to clear it with and so, thinking quickly, he'd done his best by
fetching his son's seaside bucket and spade and tried to clear it with that,
taking hours rather than minutes as a result. Manager Archie Macaulay
was not amused with Drury's explanation, but in truth, the centre-half
got off lightly – a couple of months later and he'd have been incurring the
wrath of Jimmy Hagan who would probably have had him running up
and down Ben Nevis as a punishment. During that same spell of awful
weather through early 1963, Drury was part of the Albion team which,
looking desperately for a game during a period where they only played two
competitive games between December 15th 1962 and March 2nd 1963,
took a friendly at Charlton Athletic on February 2nd in a desperate effort
to get some match practice in – though quite why they felt driving south
of the river was a good plan is anyone's guess. Whilst making their way
by coach to London, they reached Northampton when a stone shot up
off the road, completely smashed the windscreen, narrowly missing Derek
Kevan and Clive Clark who were sitting in the front seats. The driver had to
smash what was left of the windscreen to prevent it from splintering as he
was driving and so, for the rest of the journey to London, the players were
forced to huddle together to keep warm. Arriving at Charlton 20 minutes
late, cold, and not exactly in the right frame of mind for a friendly football
match, Albion's team that night were soundly beaten 5-0.

WHEREVER I LAY MY HAT

In spite of carrying off the FA Cup on five separate occasions, and reaching the final five more times besides, there have been periods where the Throstles have not enjoyed the best of fortunes in the FA Cup, especially away from The Hawthorns. Away ties were a perpetual problem through the latter part of the 20th century, for the last time Albion won an away FA Cup tie in the previous millennium was on January 23rd 1982 when they won a fourth-round game at Gillingham through a Derek Statham goal. It was almost 20 years before they broke the hoodoo, winning 2-1 at Sunderland in the third round on January 5th 2002. Replays away from The Hawthorns were more barren soil yet. After beating Nottingham Forest in a third-round second replay on the neutral ground of Filbert Street on January 29th 1973, they didn't win a replay away from the Black Country again until they beat Peterborough United 2-0 at London Road in January 2009. The last 'real' away replay they'd won stretched back even further than the Forest game – on January 11th 1971 when Albion won 3-1 at Scunthorpe United after a 0-0 draw at The Hawthorns.

Albion men have only registered three FA Cup hat-tricks in away games in the club's history. The first was scored by Joe Wilson at Chatham in the third round on March 2nd 1889 as the Throstles won 10-1, their best ever FA Cup win. Three years later on March 9th 1892, Jasper Geddes popped up with a hat-trick to decide the semi-final second-replay against Nottingham Forest as Albion won 6-3, though again, this wasn't strictly an away game given that it was played on neutral soil at Derby. The 20th century did not serve up a single FA Cup hat-trick away from The Hawthorns and we had to wait until the sixth-round tie at Bristol Rovers in 2008 when Ishmael Miller scored three in the 5-1 victory, exactly 116 years to the day after Geddes' feat.

CZECH MATES

"This morning I had another talk with the German Chancellor, Herr Hitler, and here is the paper which bears his name upon it as well as mine." The words of Britain's Prime Minister, Neville Chamberlain, on his return from the Munich summit on September 30th 1938. What was on this piece of paper? Was it the draw for the next round of the European

Cup? Was it an early version of the Bosman Ruling? Or perhaps some agreement on the number of foreign players you could put in your team for domestic games? It might as well have been any of those because, as history shows, it was one of the most worthless pieces of paper in the history of the world, about as valuable as the deeds to London Bridge, famously sold time and again to gullible American tourists with far more money than sense. What Chamberlain thought he had was a peace accord that would save Europe from a repeat of the slaughter of 1914-18. What Hitler knew he had was a neatly coded invitation to the resumption of carnage a year hence, a sequel to the Great War with the rather less snappy title of World War II. War was finally declared on September 3rd 1939, two days after Hitler had invaded Poland and Europe, and ultimately the rest of the world, was plunged into another bloody conflict that was to stretch six years into the future.

When the Great War had broken out, the Football League had tried to conduct business as usual, the 1914/15 season played out to its conclusion, in spite of the fact that war had broken out a month before the first ball was kicked. It was a decision that was greeted with great hostility, and football did not resume until well after the Armistice of November 11th 1918. The 1919/20 season heralded the return to normality, coincidentally the season when Albion won the league championship for the first and, thus far, only time. Yet while football had been suspended as a result of overwhelming public hostility back in 1915, the powers that be recognised that entertainment actually had a huge role to play in maintaining morale on the home front. While there was no appetite to maintain the existing framework of league and FA Cup competition – logistical problems made that impossible anyway – it was important that football continued to be played in some form after the Football League was abandoned three games into the 1939/40 season.

Wartime competition, in the form of cup matches and regional leagues, were quickly set up to keep clubs active, to give civilians and those still posted in the UK busy and to keep much needed revenue coming through the turnstiles. It also created an opportunity for players, both combatants and non-combatants, to continue playing throughout the hostilities. Over the war years, the Throstles were involved in several competitions, including the Midland wartime regional league, the wartime Football

League Cup, both South and North in different seasons, the Football League War Cup, and the Midland Cup – which Albion won in 1944, defeating Nottingham Forest 6-5 on aggregate in a two-legged final. Many other friendly matches were also arranged as fillers, to give some semblance of normality, and keep the minds of players and spectators alike from the horrors of war. During these troubled times, new rules of engagement, so to speak, for football competitions were adopted. Because players were, naturally enough, drafted into the services, they were no longer tied down to a specific geographic location, but were posted all over the country and from there to the theatres of war rather than the theatres of dreams.

As a result, the novel idea of clubs being able to field guest players was introduced. This rule was imposed mainly to allow players to compete with the minimum of travel hindrance, not forgetting of course that petrol rationing was in force, while any kind of travel was reduced to a minimum to give priority to the troops. So, for example, if an Albion player was posted to a military installation say in the north west, then it made more sense for that player to play locally for Manchester City, Blackburn Rovers, Liverpool or Oldham Athletic, in the event that the player be needed urgently for military purposes. Similarly, Albion could call on the services of players stationed in the Midlands, whatever their club. Over the course of the war, Albion were to field no fewer than 42 guest players, including such greats as Birmingham City's England international goalkeeper Gil Merrick, Middlesbrough's great England full-back George Hardwick, Aston Villa's Harry Parkes and Arsenal's Eddie Hapgood. Hapgood was England captain when the national side had been required to give the Nazi salute before a game with the Germans in Berlin in May 1938, a salute that Hapgood had rejected but was forced to go through with to 'avoid a diplomatic incident'. That was a humiliation well worth taking – wasn't it? – given we were bombing one another within 18 months…

To ensure football continued to be played, the Football League also sanctioned many one-off games that attracted a match fee of 30 shillings across the board for all players. The modern equivalent; a very modest £1.50. Would John Terry get out of bed – anybody's bed – for that? One of those one-offs was the Baggies' fixture against the touring Czechoslovak

Army team. Driven from their homeland by Hitler's Nazis, victims of Chamberlain's policy of appeasement back in 1938, they turned up at The Hawthorns on Saturday 1st November 1941. Their team included several Czechoslovakian internationals, who were well admired for a close passing game, a very Continental approach at that time. The Czechs were a world power in football too, having finished as runners-up to Italy in the 1934 World Cup in a tournament held under Mussolini's beady eye, the Italians apparently getting the benefit of some fairly dodgy refereeing through the competition.

Taking on the Czechs, Albion's team that day was Jimmy Adams in goal, with Idris Bassett and Cecil Shaw at full-back. The half-back line was made up of Jack Sankey, Billy Gripton and Sandy McNab. Billy Elliott occupied the right-wing berth with Sammy Heaselgrave on his inside. W. G. Richardson was at centre forward with Charles Evans and Jack Johnson on the left. Rather unusually this day, there was an Albion substitution, George Dudley, elder brother of the great Jimmy Dudley, replacing Heaselgrave, who was injured just before half-time. The *Midland Chronicle* covered the match and, in their edition of November 7th, described the Czech side's failings thus: "Though they showed cleverness and subtlety in their movements, they were not very vigorous, which put them at a disadvantage against the heavier Albion side." Their reporter continued; "Had Albion gone 'all-out' and made good use of all the chances which came their way, they would have won by a greater margin." The reporter also observed that the Czech keeper Michna was in superb form, and made many fine saves.

As it was, Albion ran out comfortable 3-1 winners. Charlie Evans scored the first after only two minutes, the ball being helped into his own net by Lorenc. The Baggies were then put on the back foot, the visitors equalising after 43 minutes, the goal coming from inside-forward Micha. It was honours even at half-time, only for Billy Elliott to restore Albion's lead almost immediately after the break, on 48 minutes. W. G. Richardson increased Albion's lead after 66 minutes, to put the game out of the reach of the tourists.

Unfortunately for them, the Czech side had come up against an Albion outfit in the middle of a run of seven Football League South wins on the trot, in which they scored a very impressive total of 47 goals, conceding only 12. Two of the victories were against our Staffordshire rivals Wolverhampton Wanderers, 8-2 at Molineux on November 8th 1941, and 5-3 at the Hawthorns the following week, which goes to show that it wasn't all bad news during the war. Two weeks later, a very unfortunate Luton Town side perished 10-1 at The Hawthorns, with W. G. Richardson bagging six of the goals. Given the shortages of raw materials, it's something of a surprise that a programme was even produced for the game. A single-sheet affair – with a crowd of just 6,280 at The Hawthorns – it's rarer still, somewhere on the level of hens' teeth, and is currently valued at anything between £100 and £150. Even the Chelsea skipper might be interested in that.

THE ONE AND ONLY

There are some records that can never be broken, notably those when the record breaker in question is first to a particular landmark. After all, nobody can now nip up Everest earlier than Hillary and Tensing can they? Nor stand on the moon before Neil Armstrong. By the side of those landmarks perhaps Jeff Astle's claim to fame – or one of them at least – is comparatively mundane, but it's his and it'll always be his. For when he put the ball past Manchester City's Joe Corrigan, later to be the Albion goalkeeping coach, in the League Cup final of 1970, Astle became the first man to have scored in both an FA Cup Final (in 1968), and a League Cup final, at Wembley Stadium.

KEEPING BUSY

Sir Alex Ferguson is often to be heard complaining about fixture pile-ups but frankly, the modern managers, they don't know they're born. You want fixture congestion? We'll give you fixture congestion. Success in particular tends to breed more and more games as you venture deeper and deeper into cup competitions, creating more and more games. Throw in a rough winter that's caused plenty of postponements and you have the 1978/79 season that should have ended with Albion drowning in a sea of silverware but finished with the Baggies empty handed. With Albion pursuing a first league title in almost 60 years, as well as the FA Cup and the Uefa Cup, the snow that blanketed the country through most of

January and February was all we needed at a time when few clubs had undersoil heating – only the likes of Liverpool could afford it. So it was in that final 84 days of the season, the Throstles played 19 First Division games, four FA Cup ties and two Uefa Cup games – a total of 25 games. No wonder they ran out of steam and ended up with nothing.

The climax to the 1967/68 season was not dissimilar, though this time the club finished up the season with their hands on the FA Cup for a fifth time. In order to do it, the final 50 days of the campaign saw the Baggies cram in ten league games and five FA Cup ties – including three against Shankly's Liverpool in the sixth round – a semi-final and the final at Wembley itself. But if you really want an example of Albion keeping themselves occupied, look no further than April 1912. Over 27 days, the Throstles played nine First Division games, an FA Cup semi-final replay which they won, an FA Cup Final against Barnsley, which ended in a 0-0 draw at Crystal Palace, and a replay of that game which Albion lost 1-0 in the final minute of extra time at Bramall Lane. After playing that original final on April 20th, Albion lost 3-0 at Everton on the 22nd, lost the FA Cup Final replay on the 24th, lost 4-1 at Blackburn on the 25th, drew 0-0 at home to Bradford City on the 26th, lost 5-1 to Sheffield Wednesday on the 27th and, after a whole day off to observe Sunday in the proper fashion, completed the campaign by drawing 0-0 at home to Oldham Athletic. Nurse, a drink for Mr Wenger! The poor chap appears to have fainted.

GLADDENED BY GLIDDEN

Tommy Glidden is one of the greatest names in Albion history, enjoying a 50-year association with the club that spanned spells as player, captain of the unique double-winning team of 1930/31, a period as coach and ultimately as a director. A true Throstle though and through, Glidden was always there in times of emergency, a thoroughly worthy successor to other great club men such as Billy Bassett and Fred Everiss. In 1964 – when manager Jimmy Hagan was in hospital for a brief period after he had reversed his car down the canal bank and into the drink at Albion's Spring Road training ground – the Baggies might have been left rudderless. But Glidden answered the call and, for a brief period, he and trainer Wilf Dixon steadied the ship and took charge of team affairs.

FANCY MEETING YOU AGAIN!

Over more than 130 years of history, the Throstles have been pitted against some clubs more than others, thanks to the vagaries of promotions, relegations and cup draws. Ironically, Wolverhampton Wanderers, Aston Villa and Birmingham City are among those we've played most regularly, much to the delight of the local constabulary. The top ten of those with whom we're most familiar is as follows:

Team	Total	Lge	FAC	LC	Oth
Wolverhampton Wanderers	156	142	11	0	3
Aston Villa	154	138	15	1	0
Everton	150	140	9	1	0
Sunderland	142	138	4	0	0
Bolton Wanderers	140	130	8	0	2
Manchester City	136	126	4	3	3
Liverpool	133	116	10	5	2
Nottingham Forest	133	114	15	3	1
Tottenham Hotspur	130	114	11	4	1
Birmingham City	126	114	8	2	2

DID YOU BACK HEEL THAT BOY?!

They also serve who only wear the shirt a few times and there have been many amongst that number over the years, perhaps more so in recent times when, particularly through the promotion season of 2003/04, a bewildering number of players represented the Throstles. It's partly to do with the changes brought about by the Bosman era no doubt, partly because of the opening up of the English game to footballers from all around the globe so that we no longer go further than Edinburgh to find talent but are happy to scour the world for it. As a consequence, pre-season games were often thick with trialists, many of whom were never seen again, while as seasons wore on in those pre-transfer-window times in Division One, Albion would still draft in yet more fresh faces. Among those was a giant Malian defender, Sekou Berthe, who came to the Albion from French club Troyes to play at the heart of the Throstles' defence, competing for places against established names such as Larus Sigurdsson and Phil Gilchrist, new hero Tommy Gaardsoe and another new face, Joost Volmer – the might of

Darren Moore was temporarily grounded after a cruciate injury sustained late in the first Premiership season.

Sekou was an imposing figure, strong and athletic, perhaps a bit on the gangly side, built as if they were constructing Peter Crouch but hadn't got all the parts in on time. He was a languid figure, a player that took his time, had his own rhythm. He could even look elegant at times. But – and it was a big but – he was very definitely a fully paid up member of the tippy tappy tendency. And we all know that tippy tappy is the father to mummy daddy football and from there… well, it's but a short step to throwing the baby out with the bathwater. He made his Albion debut in a League Cup tie at Hartlepool United and looked somewhat startled to be there and by these new surroundings, a little bit like a kitten that had been doused in petrol and given a few matches to get his claws into. He made an appearance as a sub against Millwall, then it was into the real stuff, a first league start in the ramshackle surroundings of Gillingham, a spooky day all round given that once there, we parked the car in front of a house that had a severed head in the window. Normal down there perhaps.

Anyway, Sekou strode out to do his bit as Albion cruised towards a comfortable 2-0 win that installed them at the top of the table, goals coming from Dobie and Clement. You'd think a clean sheet was a cause for celebration, but all was not well within the camp. At one juncture during the game, it was as if the world had tilted on its axis – that the very seas might be crashing in upon us – the mountains imploding. There was this guttural, full throated roar, emanating from the direction of Gary Megson. The word that he chose to tear from the bowels of his soul I cannot repeat here for there are some frontiers that the printed word still cannot cross. Suffice to say, it was sharp, crisp, choice. But it was not Gary's displeasure that remains so fresh in the forefront of the mind for hearing him give full voice to invective was not exactly a rarity, for our erstwhile manager had a full and polished vocabulary chock full with industrial-strength terms which he was rarely shy of using. The more glorious little cameo was played out at Gary's side, the place where faithful Frank Burrows stood through those tumultuous years of promotions and relegation. Always nattily attired, head swathed in flat cap, moustache bristling, brow furrowed, proud Scot Frank cut something of a military figure on the touchline. Never the austere figure

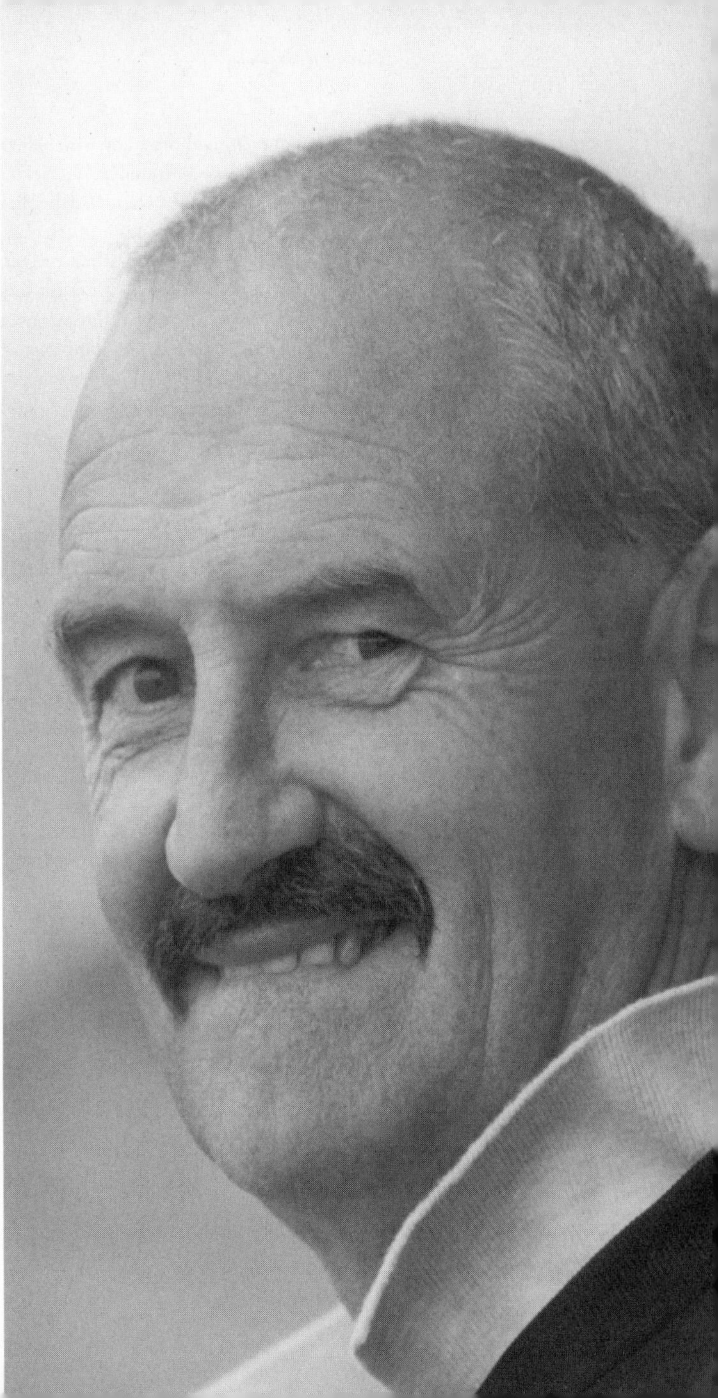

RARE SHOT OF FRANK BURROWS WITHOUT HEADGEAR

he appeared on first glance, Frank was always good company, with plenty of tales to tell about the game and a lively sense of humour. But Sekou exhausted even Frank's sense of the ridiculous. He wrenched his flat cap from his head and, in a burst of pure venom, hurled it into the dust. I cannot entirely remember what happened after that, but it's entirely possible that Frank might have jumped up and down on it, a bit like Dennis the Menace's dad. And the reason for this extraordinary chain reaction of outbursts? Sekou had suffered an unprovoked outbreak of the easy osies in his own penalty area. Amid a back five renowned for kicking the ball 60 yards first and asking questions later – much later – Sekou had committed the ultimate crime beneath the baleful gaze of his own manager. Inside his own six-yard box, under challenge, he had only gone and back-heeled the ball to a colleague. Back-heeled it! In the six-yard box! No wonder Alan Crawford dropped his notes. No, not a seismic moment in the history of the Albion, but when all's said and done, you can't beat a bit of frenzied cap tossing can you?

STRIP POKER

Though the Throstles are renowned the world over for the blue and white stripes, it wasn't until 1885 that they became the club colours. Prior to that, the club had donned an assortment of colours, such as cardinal red and blue quarters, maroon jerseys, yellow and white quarters, chocolate and blue halves and red and white hoops.

Baggies supporters first saw the use of the now traditional attire in 1885 but for some unknown reason, 1889 saw a brief return to garish colours – scarlet and blue broad stripes. Albion players very soon attracted unwanted comments and derision at the wearing of such a strip and a hasty return to blue and white stripes and white knickers was made. Since that day West Bromwich Albion Football Club has made those colours very much their own. The change colours were for many years from the 1890s a staple diet of white shirts and black shorts, but very significant changes were made on special occasions such as the 1935 FA Cup Final against Sheffield Wednesday at Wembley Stadium. Both sides had to abandon their traditional colours in favour of change, due to the clash of stripes. Albion wore blue shirts and white shorts, but it wasn't a lucky change for the club, the Baggies going down 4-2.

The status quo for all Albion kit remained much the same until 1941 when, due to shortages in the war years, striped jerseys could not be manufactured, so the 'Wembley 1935' alternative of navy shirts and white shorts was once again adopted for the duration. The Baggies did not return to the traditional blue and white stripes until the home FA Cup tie versus Leeds United on January 11th 1947. Even then, the annals of the *Albion News* shows that constant appeals were made by the club to their supporters, urging them to donate unwanted clothing coupons so that supplies of the playing kit could be maintained. From January 11th 1947 the famous blue and white livery once again terrorised away opposition at the Hawthorns, with white shirts and black shorts still the preferred change strip. Albion did stray from the norm occasionally, and, during the victorious 1953/54 campaign, against Newcastle United in the fifth round, Albion made the home change to red shirts and white shorts, with the Magpies reverting to white shirts and black shorts. History shows that the Baggies ran out 3-2 winners, thanks to a Ronnie Allen hat-trick, to take one further step towards Wembley.

At the end of the 1950s and into the early 1960s, the red away shirt was adopted. This strip was worn in one disastrous trip to Stamford Bridge in 1960, to take on Chelsea where Albion were hammered 7-1, Jimmy Greaves blasting five goals. Fast forward seven years to 1967 and even more disastrously, Albion managed to turn round a 2-0 half-time lead at Wembley against Queens Park Rangers in the League Cup final into a 3-2 defeat wearing the same all red kit. The strip was consigned to the dustbin in favour of the now famous all white Wembley 1968 kit. All red was again preferred for a short time in the 1970s until the brilliant 'Brazilian' strip of yellow with green trim and light blue shorts was adopted under the then manager Don Howe. These colours were in use until the mid 1970s when under Giles, Allen and Atkinson, green and yellow stripes with green shorts became the preferred option.

In 1982 the club launched yet another away kit, a yellow shirt with black trim and very thin pinstripes, worn with black shorts, sporting the new club sponsor logo of Swan. At the beginning of 1984/85 Albion announced a ground-breaking partnership with the local NHS and the West Midlands Health Authority, to became the first football club to promote a health issue – anti-smoking. The club shirts sported a logo, consisting of a red circle with a diagonal line across a lit cigarette. The 1986/87 season saw another curiosity, when Albion once again ran out at The Hawthorns in different colours, for the visit in a friendly fixture of Moscow Torpedo, Albion wearing their all red away strip, a change repeated against Boavista for a friendly at The Hawthorns at the start of the 2004/05 campaign.

Over the last 30 years, there have been a fair concoction of away colours, from yellow shirts with blue trim and thin blue hoops, to green and yellow pinstripe shirts with green shorts, yellow and light blue shirts with light blue shorts, bright yellow shirts with the single broad hoop across the chest and the more traditional red shirts, this time with navy shorts. We've seen Albion in blue with a diagonal sash, in white shirts and black shirts, and all yellow once again. We have seen the playing strips advance from the rugby style shirts as worn in the 1954 final, to the classic 'V' necks of the late 1950s to the crew necks of the early to mid 1960s. Thin stripes, broad stripes, medium stripes, bar code stripes. There have been oddities too. On October 2nd 1990 Albion played in an away game at Home Park, Plymouth. Neither our blue and white – nor the change green and yellow stripes – were appropriate due to a clash with the home team's green and white stripes. The supplier of the club's kit at that time was Scoreline who also had in their stable Queens Park Rangers. A set of the Rangers away strip, red and black hoops, red shorts and red socks, was hastily appropriated and worn for the only time in the 2-0 defeat to the Pilgrims. Coincidentally, when the Pilgrims came to the Hawthorns that season, the same clash ensued, but strangely, no change was made.

A similar situation occurred against Leeds United on August 19th 1972, when Albion had to don the Leeds United yellow and blue second strip, presumably because the referee wasn't happy with any of the strips that Albion had taken with them to Elland Road. Albion went down 2-0 in that match as well. Shrewsbury Town was the venue of the next significant 'out-take'. On October 6th 1981 the Baggies drew 3-3 with the Shrews in the League Cup, wearing Shrewsbury's 'all red' change strip. Finally the Baggies wore an all blue strip against Brentford in the first round, second leg of the Worthington Cup at Griffin Park on August 19th 1998. Albion went into the tie with a 2-1 lead, but suffered a 3-0 reverse in the away leg to go out of the competition. That kit was banished to the clothes rails of the club shop after only one appearance and became a very popular leisure shirt with the Albion faithful.

CROWDED HOUSE

Albion have played in front of some pretty big crowds down the years, particularly in cup finals, of course. Now then, now then, guys and gals, we have here the top ten of games what this here West Bromwich Albion have played in where the crowd has been huge. How's about that then?

May 1st 1954	Preston North End	FAC Final	Wembley	99,852
May 18th 1968	Everton	FAC Final	Wembley	99,665
Mar 7th 1970	Manchester City	LC Final	Wembley	97,963
Mar 4th 1967	Queens Park Rangers	LC Final	Wembley	97,952
Mar 7th 1979	Red Star Belgrade	UC R5 1L	Belgrade	95,300
Mar 27th 1935	Sheffield Wednesday	FAC Final	Wembley	93,204
Apr 25th 1931	Birmingham	FAC Final	Wembley	90,368
Apr 5th 2008	Portsmouth	FAC SF	Wembley	83,584
Oct 18th 2008	Manchester United	PL	Old Trafford	75,451
May 28th 2007	Derby County	Play-off Final	Wembley	74,993

Enjoy that pop pickers? Ready for the top ten league crowds? Not 'alf!

Oct 18th 2008	Manchester United	PL	Old Trafford	75,451
Dec 26th 2005	Manchester United	PL	Old Trafford	67,972
May 7th 2005	Manchester United	PL	Old Trafford	67,827
Aug 17th 2002	Manchester United	PL	Old Trafford	67,645
Oct 2nd 1954	Chelsea	D1	Stamford Br.	67,440
Oct 6th 1920	Aston Villa	D1	Villa Park	66,094
Aug 19th 1950	Aston Villa	D1	Villa Park	65,036
Mar 8th 1958	Manchester United	D1	Old Trafford	63,479
Jan 22nd 1949	Tottenham Hotspur	D2	White H. Lane	62,566
Mar 27th 1964	Everton	D1	Goodison Park	61,187

KEEPING REGULAR

Between 1957/58 and 1985/86, Albion played a competitive game against Nottingham Forest in each season, a consecutive run of 29 seasons – the longest in Albion history. The two were in the First Division together from 1957/58 to 1971/72, then met in the FA Cup the following season.

The next three seasons saw them both in Division Two and after Albion got promoted, they still met in 1976/77 in the Anglo Scottish Cup – no, Forest hadn't moved to Edinburgh, it was just a weird competition. In 1977/78, Forest rejoined Albion in the top division, the two staying there until the *annus horribilis* that was 1985/86 when the Throstles were relegated in circumstances that still make grown men weep.

TRENCH FOOTBALLER

Many footballers today sign for their new clubs in the full glare of publicity, flash bulbs popping, journalists jostling for position, TV crews documenting every moment. In years gone by, it was all rather lower key, not least in the case of Tommy Magee who signed for the Baggies while still on active service in the trenches of World War I. Tommy presumably used a shallower trench than most of his colleagues because at just 5 feet 2½ inches tall, he remains the smallest man ever to play for the Albion and, perhaps, for England too.

Born in Widnes, Magee was a talented rugby league player as a youngster before switching over to football, playing for Widnes Athletic before joining up to fight the Germans in the Great War. While on active service, his ability as a player was spotted by an Albion supporter who alerted the club to this new talent, the Throstles getting the paperwork done out in France just a few weeks after hostilities had ceased and before Magee was demobbed and returned home after the Armistice.

Magee made such a swift impression in his opening months at The Hawthorns that when league football resumed for the 1919/20 season, he was thrown straight into the first XI and went on to make a significant contribution to the campaign where the Throstles won the First Division title for the first and only time, Magee featuring in more than half the games.

The rest of the decade saw Albion endure ups and downs, ultimately ending in relegation, but in 1930/31 Magee enjoyed perhaps his greatest success at the club when he played a full part as Albion completed the unique double of winning promotion and winning the FA Cup in the same season. As a result, Magee remains the only player to have won both the league and FA Cup with the Throstles, a record that seems likely to endure for a few years yet.

IGOR OF THE ALBION

Igor Balis. Not a real Black Country name perhaps, but one that will live on for evermore for it is written in the Good Book that Igor did step up and score the injury-time penalty kick at Bradford City that won Albion promotion to the Premier League and, better yet, left Staffordshire in darkness. Darker than usual anyway. But there are so many myths and legends that surround the dark warrior from Slovakia that he might have sat around King Arthur's round table rather than Gaffer Gary's square dressing room. The international man of mystery was the very stuff of fable, yet he came so innocently and left so quietly that it's almost as if he had never really been here, were it not for those footprints left in the Black Country swarf, and the slew of kids who represented a spike in the birth rate, all conceived in the fumbling throes of post-Bradford booze-soaked ecstasy and who now bear his name in memory of that great day in Yorkshire.

It's easy to forget that Igor arrived the season before his great glory, coming to The Hawthorns on trial before Christmas 2000 before signing up as a player. These were the days before we had our own training ground, when footballers reported to the dressing rooms in Halfords Lane before finding out where they were going to go training, generally finding themselves on the patch of grass behind the Tom Silk Building. In the morning, it was a regular sight on the Birmingham Road to see Igor walking purposefully towards The Hawthorns with his boots in a brown paper parcel under his arm. Unless he was bringing in the empties for recycling – Igor gained something of a reputation while billeted in the Moat House of giving the mini bar in his room some 'ammer. This quickly stopped when he realised he had to pay for said drinks and had already used up most of his relocation allowance. Actually, the contents of the mini bar were possibly a little tame for Igor. When he was joined later by Stanislav Varga at the Shrine, the two were able to drink Andy Johnson under the table by the use of strange, blue vodka (possibly meths, though we could never substantiate this). Getting Jonno hammered was no small feat but the Slovaks did it with ease.

Once he was properly signed up here, the Balis family was ferried over to join him, including the kids, Boris and Denis. Another indelible memory of the Balis years was seeing him in the car park in Halfords Lane after a game, sitting in his car like a particularly high powered KGB agent – yes, I know it's the wrong nationality – the window wound halfway down so you could just see his penetrating gaze. As he sat, he threw a tennis ball into the distance for Denis and Boris to fetch. Well, he wasn't allowed to keep a dog in the house he was renting.

But then – the day of days – Bradford. Gary Megson has allowed the legend to grow that, in that season, where we couldn't score a penalty for love nor money, Igor had never told anybody he could take them. Clearly nonsense for a manager who so prided himself on attention to detail would surely not have failed to notice that in the early season League Cup shoot-out at Cambridge United, Igor was one of those who slotted his spot kick away with aplomb. There again, the best penalty of the night was converted by James Quinn, so go figure. The other tale, that Igor was the only one willing to take the penalty because he was the only one who had no idea of its significance, is equally daft. Igor might not have had a Shakespearean command of the Queen's English, but he was well capable of reading a league table. And nor was he anybody's fool. Igor knew more English than he ever let on, a neat tactic to help him avoid being quizzed by the media. He was rumbled one day when padding down the corridor from restaurant to the dressing room. We caught him lustily trumpeting the virtues of fish and chips with Varga. The look on his face when he saw he'd been overheard was priceless. But some secrets are best kept in house and we chose never to expose Igor's blossoming grasp of English. One more season was Igor's lot in England, then he returned home. I'd like to think there are whole sections of Bratislava that have been renamed in his honour, for that might be some compensation for the fact that the international man of mystery now struggles with tinnitus. Where he got it, who knows. Mind, it was noisy work being a full-back patrolling up and down in front of that dug out.

ON THE BEACH

Footballers can be a pretty insular bunch, not looking much further than the end of their noses and the end of the week. The game is so intense that there's often little time to look beyond next Saturday and doing your particular job for the team, so much so that even basic geography can escape their grasp. So it was with Doug Fraser, league and FA Cup winner with the Throstles during the 1960s. The wing-half, who was later converted to full-back, joined the Albion from Aberdeen and Doug was every bit as tough as the granite on which his native city was built, a real hard man. He must have been because it was his regular habit to take a dip in the North Sea. Anybody who has ever spent time in Aberdeen knows only too well that even in the midst of a sweltering summer, you rarely strip down beyond the thermals up there, so Fraser was of hardy stock. Playing in the same Aberdeen side as Charlie Cooke, who made the move to Chelsea, it was inevitable that he would eventually make a move to England too and it was Albion boss Jimmy Hagan who secured his signature. Shacked up in a West Bromwich hotel after making the switch, clearly Doug hadn't wasted too much time in consulting his atlas to find out just where he was moving to. On his first morning in the Black Country, he bounded down to reception, towel slung over his shoulder and demanded; "Which is the best way to the beach?"

WHISTLER'S BOTHER

Although the first FA Cup Final at Wembley was contested between West Ham United and Bolton Wanderers back in 1923, an Albion man played a key role in the legendary 'White Horse Final'.

The referee that day was David Asson, already a whistler of some repute having already officiated at the game between the Football League and the Scottish League at Highbury two years earlier. He was appointed a league linesman in 1912 – and ran the line at the 1922 FA Cup Final – and had been given the nod to referee league football in 1914. He was given the chance to ref that first Wembley final and had to call on all his experience as the pitch first had to be cleared by the white police horse for the game to then be played, with spectators right up against the pitch markings. The Albion connection? Asson only embarked on a career as a referee after his hopes of becoming a professional footballer with the Throstles were dashed. He joined the Albion on July 2nd 1898 and had one season on the club's books before being released. He never played for the first team, but at least he played at Wembley before Albion did.

DOUBLE AGENTS

Albion's closest rivalry, certainly in the club's earliest years, was with the team from Witton Lane – Aston Villa. In spite of that, more than 30 players have been involved at both football clubs which makes them either brave or barmy. You decide…

Darren Bradley was an apprentice pro with Villa and came to Albion as part of the deal that took Steve Hunt to Villa Park. He stayed for nine years, captained the club to play-off victory and scored one of the all-time great Albion goals against the Wolves.

John Crisp was a Villa trialist, who joined Albion in 1914. He served in the Royal Navy during World War I before returning to The Hawthorns where he won a league championship medal before moving on to Blackburn Rovers in 1923.

Jimmy Cumbes was a jack of all trades, playing first-class cricket for Lancashire and Worcestershire, fronting a radio show for Radio Birmingham and keeping goal for both the Albion and then Villa after his move to the Baggies from Tranmere Rovers.

Curtis Davies was another who skippered the Albion, this time before changing his allegiance and heading for Villa Park in return for a fee of around £9 million.

John Deehan joined Albion from Villa after Ron Atkinson was faced with a striking crisis following a knee injury to Cyrille Regis. Deehan never really found his best form at The Hawthorns and left for Norwich City after a couple of years with the Baggies.

Jimmy Dugdale was one of those rare footballers who not only won two FA Cup winners' medals, but did it with different clubs; Albion in 1954 and Villa in 1957.

Lloyd Dyer was a former Villa apprentice who moved to The Hawthorns in 2001 and ultimately became the talisman for the 2003/04 promotion-winning team, turning a number of games Albion's way with his blistering pace.

Ugo Ehiogu was pinched for the Villa by former Albion boss Ron Atkinson who lured his away from The Hawthorns when he was still a junior professional. Ehiogu almost returned in January 2006 before a transfer deal fell through.

Albert Evans was a former Villa full-back who signed for the Throstles in 1907 and then coached the first team following his 1909 retirement.

Graham Fenton's spell at The Hawthorns was short and sweet, the youngster making a huge impression during a brief loan spell in the Black Country in 1994. He didn't fulfil his potential at Villa Park and was soon on his way from there.

William Garraty turned pro as a youngster at Villa Park and returned there as the club's trainer after finishing his career. In between times, he had spells at Leicester Fosse, and then the Albion.

Andy Gray was a Scottish international who found fame in the Midlands, first with Villa before moving to Wolves for a then record fee of £1.5 million, a figure eclipsed when Bryan Robson left Albion for Manchester United. Gray atoned for those sins by joining Albion in 1987. Take a bow, son.

Harry Hadley became a professional at Stoney Lane in 1897 and played 181 games for the Throstles, as well as playing for England before moving to the Villa in 1905.

George Holden had already guested for the Albion in 1883 before he joined Villa in 1885 from Wednesbury Old Athletic. He returned to the Baggies as an amateur a year later.

Robert Hopkins was another who did the rounds of the Midlands clubs, taking in Albion, Villa and Birmingham City during a career as an aggressive midfield presence.

Steve Hunt was unusual in that he really made his reputation as a player in the United States, playing for New York Cosmos – Pele, Beckenbauer and all – in the NASL in the late 1970s. He joined Albion from Coventry in 1984 and then switched to Villa Park two years later, having played for England while at The Hawthorns.

Mark Kinsella was at the end of his career when he joined Albion from Villa to help them get over the promotion line in 2004. The Irish international's most successful years were perhaps those he spent at Charlton Athletic.

Arthur Loach turned professional with Albion in 1885 and joined Villa just 12 months later after scoring nine goals in just 14 games.

Ken McNaught joined Albion in 1983 after being a key member of the successful Villa side of the late 1970s and early 1980s where he formed a strong centre-half partnership with Allan Evans, who later joined the Albion coaching staff.

Luke Moore made a £3 million move up Island Road to The Hawthorns in 2007 after establishing himself as an England under-21 in his time at Villa Park.

Tony Morley played a major role in the winning of the European Cup for the Villa before joining Albion towards the end of his career in 1987, serving under former Villa boss Ron Saunders. Moving swiftly on…

Jesse Pennington, now inextricably linked with Albion folklore, started his career as an amateur at Villa but they didn't think he'd make it and allowed him to join Albion where he played almost 500 games, skippered the title-winning team of 1919/20, and won 25 England caps.

Cyrille Regis was catapulted to prominence at The Hawthorns after being plucked from non-league obscurity at Hayes in 1977, making over 300 appearances for Albion. He ended up at Villa Park 14 years later, before returning to The Hawthorns where he was first-team coach under the management of former Villa striker Brian Little.

Bob Roberts joined Albion upon the club's formation and became its first England international. The goalkeeper joined Villa in 1892 before wisely deciding to retire a year later.

Riccardo Scimeca turned professional at Villa before making a big money move to Nottingham Forest in 1999. He joined Albion in May 2004 and became a part of the 'Great Escape' team of 2004/05.

Nigel Spink was the hero of Aston Villa's European Cup win in 1982, coming on as a sub for the injured Jimmy Rimmer early in the game. He joined Albion in 1996 and played 24 times for the club.

Kenny Swain joined Villa from Chelsea in 1978 having had a loan spell at The Hawthorns earlier that year. He came back on loan later when he was at Portsmouth.

Garry Thompson joined Albion from Coventry City in 1983 and after scoring 45 goals in 105 games, moved on to Sheffield Wednesday in 1985 and then Villa a year later.

Andy Townsend reached The Hawthorns at a stage in his career where the mind was certainly willing but the flesh had pretty much given up. Earlier in his career, the Irish international gave Villa sterling service.

Dave Walsh became one of Albion's greatest goalscorers after joining from Linfield in the aftermath of World War II, scoring 100 goals in 174 games, helping Albion to promotion in 1948/49 before joining Villa 18 months later.

Gavin Ward played just one game in goal for Albion having begun his career at Villa Park. He later moved to Cardiff City.

George Wheldon had a trial with Albion in May 1890 and later ended up at Villa in 1896. He eventually returned to the Baggies, signing in 1900.

Jimmy Williams was a winger who joined Albion from Villa in 1905 before he moved on to Brownhills Albion after playing 35 games for the Throstles.

Joe Wilson joined Albion from Walsall Town in 1887 after starting his career at the Villa. He had an extraordinary FA Cup record, scoring 12 times in 13 ties, and another in a tie with Accrington that was later declared null and void.

THE LAST TIME

The Albion moved into The Hawthorns in 1900 and have stayed there ever since, much as the old place has changed. Many a club, though, has moved away from its traditional home and into plusher new premises, particularly over the last 20 years or so since the disasters at Bradford and Hillsborough and the improvements to ground safety that were rightly demanded in their aftermath. When did Albion last visit some grand old grounds?

Club	Venue	Date	Result
Arsenal	Highbury	April 15th 2006	1-3
Bolton Wanderers	Burnden Park	March 2nd 1997	0-1
Bradford PA	Park Avenue	November 20th 1948	1-4
Brighton & HA	Goldstone Ground	March 20th 1991	0-2
Bristol Rovers	Eastville Stadium	May 12th 1979	3-2
Cardiff City	Ninian Park	April 1st 2008	0-0
Chester City	Sealand Road	October 7th 1939	2-0
Colchester United	Layer Road	October 20th 2007	2-3
Coventry City	Highfield Road	December 20th 2003	0-1
Darlington	Feethams	August 24th 1991	1-0
Derby County	Baseball Ground	January 2nd 1995	1-1
Doncaster Rovers	Belle Vue	January 5th 1957	1-1
Huddersfield Town	Leeds Road	August 22nd 1992	1-0
Hull City	Boothferry Park	October 31st 1992	2-1
Leicester City	Filbert Street	January 1st 1991	1-2
Manchester City	Maine Road	February 1st 2003	2-1
Middlesbrough	Ayresome Park	September 14th 1994	1-2
Millwall	The Den	September 10th 1994	2-2
Newport County	Somerton Park	August 3rd 1984	1-2
Northampton Town	County Ground	January 28th 1967	3-1
Oxford United	Manor Ground	September 20th 1998	0-3
Reading	Elm Park	December 26th 1997	1-2
Rotherham United	Millmoor	October 25th 2003	3-0
Scunthorpe United	The Old Showground	January 11th 1971	3-1
Shrewsbury Town	Gay Meadow	May 2nd 1992	3-1
Southampton	The Dell	January 1st 1986	1-3
Stoke City	Victoria Ground	May 4th 1997	1-2
Sunderland	Roker Park	April 27th 1996	2-2

Swansea City .... The Vetch Field .... May 16th 1993 1-2
Walsall .... Fellows Park .... August 18th 1986 2-2
Wigan Athletic .... Springfield Park .... October 17th 1992 0-1
Wimbledon .... Plough Lane .... January 9th 1988 1-4

WHERE AND WHEN

As founder members of the Football League, it's only right and proper that the Throstles have spent the bulk of their seasons ensconced within England's top flight, 72 of them up to the end of the 2009/10 campaign. So where were we, and when?

Premiership

1888/89 to 1900/01	13 seasons
1902/03 to 1903/04	2 seasons
1911/12 to 1926/27	12 seasons
1931/32 to 1937/38	7 seasons
1949/50 to 1972/73	24 seasons
1976/77 to 1984/85	10 seasons
2002/03	1 season
2004/05 to 2005/06	2 seasons
2008/09	1 season

Championship

1901/02	1 season
1904/05 to 1910/11	7 seasons
1927/28 to 1930/31	4 seasons
1938/39 to 1948/49	4 seasons
1973/74 to 1975/76	3 seasons
1985/86 to 1990/91	6 seasons
1993/94 to 2001/02	9 seasons
2003/04	1 season
2006/07 to 2007/08	2 seasons
2009/10	1 season

League One

1991/92 to 1992/93	2 seasons

UNKNOWN PLEASURES

Though Albion seem to have been here, there and everywhere over recent years, for the dedicated groundspotter there are still a few stadia where, up to the end of 2009/10, the Throstles have yet to boldly go…

Accrington Stanley.. Fraser Eagle Stadium
Aldershot Town... EBB Stadium
Brighton & Hove Albion .... The Withdean Stadium
Boston United .... York Street Stadium
Burton Albion ....Pirelli Stadium
Colchester United .... Weston Home Community Stadium
Darlington .... Balfour Webnet Arena
Dagenham & Redbridge .... Victoria Road
Macclesfield Town .... Moss Rose Stadium
Milton Keynes Dons... MK Stadium
Morecambe ....Christie Park
Rochdale ....Spotland
Rotherham United.. Don Valley Stadium

THE UNDEFEATED

Over the course of Albion's league history, dating back to their role as founder members of the Football League in 1888/89, the club has twice posted a record of 17 games unbeaten. The first came in 1901/02 as the club looked to rebuild from the ashes of a first-ever relegation the season before. Second Division football clearly suited them as the Throstles swept to immediate promotion, as champions to boot. They started the season strongly enough, but got better and better after their second defeat came in game 12 of the season, losing 2-0 at Doncaster Rovers. That result clearly concentrated a few minds and the Baggies reeled off an amazing ten straight wins, starting off at Burton United 3-1. Then there were four at The Hawthorns – over Lincoln City 4-1, Middlesbrough 2-0, Barnsley 3-1 and Stockport County 3-0 – before recording an away victory at Leicester Fosse, on December 28th 1901. Into 1902 and Albion then recorded victories at Preston North End 2-1, at home to Leicester Fosse 1-0, and Burnley 3-0, before travelling to Burslem Port Vale to win 3-2. Gainsborough Trinity spoilt the trend by getting a 1-1 draw but it was back to winning ways at Bristol City 2-1. The Baggies then extended that winning streak to five with a 7-2 thrashing of Blackpool, a 2-0 victory at Stockport County and a 4-0 home win over Newton Heath (better known today as Manchester United), before winning 2-1 at Glossop. Albion shared the spoils 2-2 at home to Doncaster Rovers before, with promotion all but sealed, they finally tasted defeat, 1-0 at Lincoln City. They'd had 119 days without defeat; played 17, won 15, drawn two, scored 47, conceded 13.

Albion then recorded a similar run of results in the 1957/58 season on their way to fourth place in the First Division. After taking four points from the first four games, Albion clicked into gear, starting with a 4-1 victory over Preston North End at The Hawthorns on September 7th 1957. A 2-2 draw away to Chelsea was followed by a fine 2-1 away win at Hillsborough. Another draw against Chelsea at the Hawthorns, 1-1, was followed by the record thumping of Manchester City 9-2, once again at home. A 2-0 away win at Nottingham Forest's City Ground, always a 'bogey' ground for Albion, was followed by a tight 0-0 draw at home to neighbours Birmingham City. Portsmouth were next to leave the Hawthorns empty handed after a 3-1 defeat, but Bolton then held Albion to a 2-2 draw, again at the Hawthorns. A 1-1 draw at Elland Road, Leeds, was followed by a fine 4-3 victory over the 'Busby Babes' of Manchester United, whose visit to the Hawthorns was the last for so many of their fine young players, so tragically lost at Munich. Following the win over United, Albion travelled to Everton to record a very creditable 1-1 draw, before returning home to defeat Aston Villa 3-2. Derek Kevan's equaliser against Wolves secured a 1-1 draw at Molineux, a prelude to a fine 3-0 home win over Sunderland. A Bobby Robson double helped Albion to a 3-3 draw at Filbert Street, Leicester, before the same player grabbed a 55th-minute equaliser at home to Blackpool on December 7th, where the great run was to end after Blackpool scored the fastest goal of the campaign at the Hawthorns, netting after just 55 seconds. The following week, December 14th, Albion travelled to Kenilworth Road, Luton, where Robson's goal was the only highlight of their 5-1 defeat, at the hands of the 'Hatters'. This was to be Albion's highest reverse of the campaign. What a way to end a record run.

FIRING BLANKS

Scoring goals away from home is never easy, but from a time in 1923, it seemed as if the Throstles had changed their name to West Bromwich Albion Nil. After they got a 1-1 draw at Nottingham Forest's City Ground in the first away fixture of the 1923/24 campaign, the Baggies then went ten successive away games without troubling the scorers, collecting a mere four points over that period. The hoodoo was finally broken just after Christmas at Manchester City's Maine Ground as the Albion went berserk and scored three, Joe Carter scoring twice, Sid Bowser adding the other. Even then, Albion only managed a draw. In the remaining nine away games that Albion played that season, they reverted to type and were scoreless in six of the final nine fixtures, ending up with the grand total of eight goals in 21 matches away from God's country.

TESTING, TESTING

You might think that the play-offs are an invention of comparatively recent times, but there really is nothing new under the sun. The Throstles were embroiled in play-off football as far back as 1896, although back then they were called test matches. Perhaps they were more sensible back then, for they involved a team from the bottom of Division One – Albion on that occasion – playing a round-robin against the top two from Division Two, the top two teams getting to play in the top flight the following year. Their opponents that year were Liverpool and Manchester City, very much junior sides compared with the Throstles at that stage of the game, twice the FA Cup winners and founder members of the Football League. Albion had finished the league season with just 19 points from 30 matches and they embarked on this crucial series of fixtures by drawing 1-1 in Manchester, then sweeping City aside 6-1 at Stoney Lane. With their First Division status all but secured, Albion could survive a 2-0 defeat in Liverpool, winning the return game by the same score and staying in the top flight.

It was almost a century before the Albion were embroiled in another test match, the promotion play-offs of 1992/93. Under Ossie Ardiles, Albion's swaggering, exciting brand of attacking football saw them finish fourth in Division Two and they were pitted against Swansea City in the semi-final as a result. A 2-1 defeat in teeming rain at the Vetch was a great result for a below-par Baggies and they comfortably recovered the position on a pulsating night that has entered Albion folklore, the Throstles winning 2-0 back at The Hawthorns, thereby earning the right to play Port Vale at Wembley where Albion won a comfortable 3-0 victory to seal promotion. The Baggies were in the play-offs again in 2000/01 after finishing sixth in the league, but despite leading Bolton Wanderers 2-0 with 10 minutes of the first leg of the semi-final remaining, Bolton snuck a 2-2 draw at The Hawthorns and then won 3-0 back at the Reebok to condemn Albion to another season in the First Division. Albion's most recent brush with the play-offs came after finishing fourth in the Championship in 2006/07. Albion were pitted against Wolves and took them apart at Molineux before finishing the job at The Hawthorns, winning 4-2 on aggregate. Derby County were the opponents for the club's first appearance at the new Wembley, an unhappy occasion as the Throstles lost out to the game's only goal.

BUDDY CAN YOU SPARE A DIME?

In spite of football being awash with cash these days, plenty of clubs are finding it hard to make ends meet. Albion aren't one of them, but away back in 1904, the club found itself on the brink of extinction as its finances were in tatters. Following relegation from the First Division at the end of the 1903/04 season, there was plenty of discontent. Jem Bayliss was re-elected as chairman, but he and his fellow directors soon found themselves in the midst of a crisis.

Falling gate receipts following relegation – Albion's average attendance that season was a pathetic 4,484 – allied to very poor performances on the pitch, helped to exacerbate matters and when the 'Noah's Ark' stand was destroyed by fire in the November of 1904, the club's future looked very bleak. The club issued a circular stating that all Albion players were available for transfer. That would have been extremely unsettling for the playing staff, who had already agreed to play for half their normal wages to help keep the club afloat. Unfortunately, this did not stem the crisis and in December, Bayliss faced the very real prospect of closing the club down.

In January of 1905, the crisis came to a head when the *Sporting Chronicle* reported the danger of Albion being wound-up, which set alarm bells

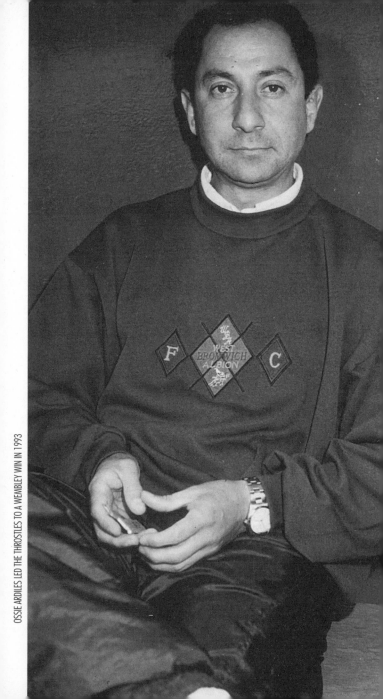

OSSIE ARDILES LED THE THROSTLES TO A WEMBLEY WIN IN 1993

ringing amongst all the club's major creditors who started to press the club for payment of outstanding bills, and the club's bankers, Parr's Bank Limited, issued a writ for the overdraft which had been run up. Over the following weeks and months, the club's solicitors were engaged in countless meetings with creditors and debenture holders to try to resolve the financial plight that the club were in; winding up looked inevitable. Mr Taylor, the club auditor, showed that in the preceding nine months, £861 had been lost, and total expenses, including the players' wages, amounted to £3,564. Taylor asked all creditors, including the bank, if they could forego their claims on monies owed until the club regained its First Division status. Not a healthy option, but the motion was accepted, and for the time being at least, Albion were saved.

However, the drama was not over, and on March 6th 1905, the now historic EGM took place, at The Hawthorns Hotel. The entire board resigned, and the new four-man leadership team was elected to steer Albion through the stormy waters of the coming years. Billy Bassett was elected yet again as a director along with Mr Spencer and Mr Couse, with Harry Keys (who was not at the meeting), elected as chairman. A new financial advisory committee was formed at the same time.

In the coming months and years the new board, with the inspirational Harry Keys and Billy Bassett at the helm, would slowly turn the club around. At the end of the April, the club and the new board received assistance from the editor of the *Birmingham Gazette, Evening Despatch* and *Sports Argus*, William McAleice, who on behalf of the club issued an appeal to his readers in a desperate attempt to raise further funding and secure the immediate, short-term future of the football club, giving the directors time to regroup and develop a strategy to take things forward into the future on a more sustainable basis. Arguing that the new board were the men to lead the club to a brighter future, he urged all well-wishers to contribute to a 'Shilling Fund' which was being launched in association with the newspapers. "Every farthing will be devoted to give the club a new life, and all contributions will be duly acknowledged in the papers named."

The Shilling Fund was an enormous success and without doubt saved the Albion. The chairman of Mitchell & Butlers Brewery, William Waters, generously opened the fund with a donation of 'Five Hundred

Shillings'. Other donations were received from Kidderminster Harriers (147 shillings), Hudson's Soap Works (80s), John Lewis of Blackburn (75/6s), Lightwoods FC (84s), West Bromwich Wednesbury Athletic Club (63s), and finally Aston Villa Football Club with a magnificent gesture of 50 shillings. A £50 cheque was also received from Newcastle United Football Club, which probably summed up the esteem in which West Bromwich Albion was held, in the football world.

All sorts of fundraising events were organised to support the fund, which culminated in the magnificent sum of £401 11s 6d being handed to the club in October of 1905. From then on it was a slow but successful recovery culminating, eventually, with promotion, as champions back to the First Division, at the end of the 1910/11 campaign.

INTO THE NEW MILLENNIUM

Daryl Burgess had the honour of scoring Albion's final goal of the 20th century when he netted against Bolton Wanderers at the Reebok Stadium in a 1-1 draw on December 28th 1999. We waited with expectation to see who would be the first scorer of the new millennium. And waited. And waited. That historic goal did not arrive until four games in when, on January 29th 2000, Lee Hughes scored a penalty in a 1-1 draw with Swindon Town at The Hawthorns as Albion became embroiled in a run of 12 league games without a win. Hughes had also scored the final Albion Hawthorns goal of the previous century in the 2-2 FA Cup draw with Blackburn Rovers on December 11th 1999. The Throstles weren't exactly rapid in ushering in the 20th century either – they had to wait for Harry Hadley to score in the 2-0 win over Burnley on January 20th 1900 to score a first goal in the New Year.

RIGHT SAID FRED

At the conclusion of the 1908/09 season two Albion juniors, Tom Robson, left-back and captain, and Henry Ellis, centre-half, were selected for the England Juniors international against Scotland in Glasgow. Secretary Fred Everiss was assigned to accompany the party to Scotland, a trip which so nearly had disastrous consequences. Their train was derailed at Crawford in Lanarkshire, whilst travelling at 50 miles per hour and Mr Everiss was trapped in one of the carriages. He managed to kick himself out of the upturned carriage and released himself from the wreck which lay directly in the path of the oncoming London to Glasgow express train. It continued a tough time for Everiss who, along with Harry Keys and Dan Nurse, had guaranteed funds of around £420, not an insubstantial amount in those days, to cover players' wages and expenses to keep Albion afloat. These financial problems, his workaholic attitude to keeping the club going and then this very serious accident, all combined to cause him serious health problems. In fact, he resigned from his post in April 1910 for a short period of three months, whilst his health improved. His soon to be brother-in-law, Ephraim Smith, stepped in to look after things whilst Fred was away. He recovered sufficiently to resume his duties at the start of the 1910/11 season.

A VERY NICE MAN

Those of us who follow the Albion, over land and sea – and water – will all have our horror stories about nightmare journeys, delays, breakdowns and the like, but even the great and the good have had their moments. Back in his early days at the club, Tony Brown and fellow youngster Gerry Howshall decided it'd be a good plan to head off to watch England under-23s play the Welsh at Wrexham. On their way back, the fanbelt snapped in Howshall's car and, given that neither were wearing tights, they had nothing to fix it with – and the café services that they'd managed to pull into was closed to boot. They called out the AA and waited. And waited. And waited. Desperate for a drink, parked next to a coffee machine, but without a sixpence between them to get one. Eventually, after two and a half hours, the AA man turned up, full of apologies – he'd broken down as well. The pair finally rolled in home at 4.30 that morning, ready to get up for training under Jimmy Hagan the following day. Professional football, it's all glamour.

THE MILLS BOMB

There used to be a time when £516,000 was a lot of money as opposed to John Terry's spare change after a night out. For a football transfer, there was a brief moment when that number represented the record fee paid between two British clubs. More remarkable yet, it was the Albion who inscribed the cheque for the appropriate amount. Albion first breached the half a million barrier and sent shockwaves through the game of football. Until, a couple

of weeks later, Brian Clough decided to take tricky Trev from Birmingham City to the Tricky Trees of Nottingham Forest for roughly twice as much money and Albion's heroics were totally forgotten. Which is roughly what happened to David Mills, the man who was briefly the most expensive footballer in England before he found himself the unfortunate victim of one of those transfers that just doesn't work out.

Mills had the most thankless of tasks from the outset, Middlesbrough's attacking midfielder coming to the Black Country billed as the new Tony Brown, about as easy a job as being the Second Coming, though at least Mills escaped the Midlands without ever being nailed to anything. Albion boss Ron Atkinson was following the dictum that it's always wise to improve your team from a position of strength, something Liverpool had long turned into a fine art under Bill Shankly and Bob Paisley. The Throstles hadn't been in such a strong position in years, for this was January 1979 and the club were about to perch ourselves atop the First Division.

The acquisition of Mills didn't look like a bad bit of business as it happened because he had shown a knack for knocking in goals at Ayresome Park over the years and with Bomber approaching the end of his career, Big Ron's decision to think ahead looked shrewd. Except nobody had told Bomber that he was approaching the end. He carried on playing well and scoring goals through to the end of the 1978/79 campaign while Mills fretted on the bench in the days when you had just a single substitute rather than a jury of them. Weeks and weeks passed and the new boy got barely a sniff of the action, the anticipation building, supporters getting increasingly feverish at the prospect of seeing him tear up the opposition and fire us to the title. To make it worse, this was the winter of our discontent, snow falling from the sky in great white lumps for days on end, postponing game after game, leaving our season becalmed while Liverpool, with their undersoil heating, carried on playing. Perhaps we should have used the £516,000 on that instead.

Albion could feel the season slipping away from them, supporters choked by the loss of an historic moment, the promise of a first league title in 59 years. And when you're desperate, you turn to your big names and, at half a million quid's worth, David Mills was our big player. Only he couldn't find any form. The weight of expectations; the expectations of the wait, nerves, the weather that took our rhythm away, or simply a case of being in the wrong place at the wrong time. Whatever it was, nothing worked for David Mills. It didn't help that he was nearly five times more expensive than any other player in that side, that the contrast between £516,000 Mills and £5,000 Cyrille could not have been more marked. But at The Hawthorns, Mills was the man with the anti-Midas touch. Everything upon which he laid a boot turned to dust. His 15 minutes of fame were transformed to four years of infamy as supporters turned on him for not being the player they thought £516,000 represented. In Albion folklore, Mills has gone down as a major misfit, a harsh reflection on a player who worked hard, tried and tried, but for whom it was never going to work. At £100,000, he'd have been a solid enough investment. But players don't write their own price tags.

THE ITALIAN JOB

With Roberto Di Matteo at the helm as head coach, Albion have gone all Continental these days – what would Teddy Sandford have thought of dishing up cappuccinos instead of cuppas at his old cafe next to the ground? But Di Matteo is not the first Italian influence at The Hawthorns, for in the late 1990s two gentlemen of Verona – or somewhere in Italy anyway – arrived in West Bromwich. Mario Bortolazzi came to the Black Country as minder to the young Enzo Maresca and spent a year in the Midlands without ever getting the hang of the lawnmower. It's a long story. As was the grass in the finish. As a footballer, there was a certain Italian finesse and elegance to Mario, even if he had left his best football on the playing fields of Serie A, most notably the San Siro in two spells with Milan much earlier in his career, the ability that had taken him to those heady heights still very apparent in his touch and vision. Nonetheless, he was still a tidy, cultured player in the Albion midfield, a midfield that took on a remarkably cosmopolitan look that year with Mario's compatriot Maresca, the Dutch master, Richard Sneekes, and the all-round renaissance man, Sean Flynn. In spite of a string of niggling injuries that hampered him and restricted his contribution to the cause, in the course of that 1998/99 campaign, Mario mustered 25 league starts and 10 more substitute appearances. He registered two goals for the Throstles, the first the meat in a Sean Murphy/Lee Hughes sandwich as we beat Port Vale 3-2 on Boxing Day 1998, the second coming just three weeks later, giving us the lead at Carrow Road before Norwich grabbed a 1-1 draw.

With Maresca acclimatised and increasingly taking Mario's starting place in the team, Bortolazzi returned home in the summer of 1999, playing for Livorno where he later started his coaching career, ending up on the Italian management team for Euro 2008. Italy were certainly cursed with ill fortune at Euro 2008, first losing Fabio Cannavaro to injury before the tournament, then, as they progressed to the knockout stages, losing Andrea Pirlo and Gennaro Gattuso to suspension. That led to Donadoni and his think-tank abandoning the more attack-minded instincts that have been part of Italy's evolution in the last two years, opting for a defensive policy that saw them to a penalty shoot-out with Spain, which was lost. A missed penalty kick saw Donadoni and his team swept out of office for the return of Marcello Lippi, the coach who won the World Cup with Italy in 2006. Maybe Mario might get his boots out again, for he still has the touch as a player, exporting an Albion game to training sessions with the Azzurri. In training sessions at Euro 2008, the Italians played a variant on the football bowls game in which Joe Corrigan reigns supreme at The Hawthorns, Mario regularly coming out on top against the likes of Antonio Cassano. You can take the boy out of the Albion, but you can't take the Albion out of the boy...

ICE COLD IN ALBION

The big freeze in the winter of 1963 totally wiped out football for weeks after Christmas, well into January and February. Desperate for football, Albion were one of the few clubs who tried everything within their power to get matches played. On one such occasion, January 12th 1963, the Baggies were scheduled to play a home fixture against Sheffield Wednesday. For the best part of a week leading up to the game, Albion had a 40-strong team working around the clock to clear the pitch of the snow and ice that formed and reformed. Tons of Southport sand was spread over the playing surface, too, and the cost of this pre-match preparation was believed to be in the region of £500, not a small amount of cash back in the early 1960s, given that an average weekly wage would have been around £8. Despite this, the state of the pitch prior to the game was "laughable" according to Ron Springett, the Sheffield Wednesday keeper. However, the referee, Mr Hamer from Bolton, obviously disagreed and he passed the pitch fit to play.

Sheffield Wednesday then went about giving a cumbersome Albion side the run-around, a real football lesson as some scribes of the day reported. David 'Bronco' Layne opened Wednesday's account as early as the second minute, and the visitors continued to frustrate Albion for the rest of the first half. Derek Kevan had one of those days when nothing would go right. The big man saw at least four good chances go begging, with the Albion faithful starting to get irritated. In the second period, Wednesday again started the better and it wasn't long before Quinn got their second. In the 70th minute, full-back Johnson added the third, and it was all over, a disappointing day for all at the club; the players, the fans of course, and the board, having to lay out all that cash for little or no reward, other than a bit of match practice for the team. The game against Sheffield Wednesday was the only league game that Albion managed to play between the 3-0 win over Manchester United on December 15th 1962 and the 2-1 defeat at Tottenham Hotspur on March 2nd 1963, a period of 11 weeks. The only other senior competitive game they managed over that period was the 5-1 FA Cup third-round win at Plymouth Argyle. Albion played 21 games in the final 78 days of the season to fulfil the fixture list.

I GET UP, I GET DOWN...

Albion have experienced the 'highs' and 'lows' of promotion and relegation on 20 occasions, 10 apiece. In 1888/89, on formation of the new Football League, Albion were invited to become one of the founder members and remained a top-flight side until relegation to Division Two in 1900/01. After one season in the second tier, Albion returned from whence they came as champions in 1901/02, but just two seasons later, it was time for the dreaded drop again.

In 1910/11, Albion returned to the First Division as champions, and there they remained until 1926/27, when they were relegated again. It was, of course, a stay at the top sadly interrupted by the ravages of war, from 1914-1918, when the league was suspended. On return to football action, the Baggies created history by winning their only First Division title. Sadly, after 12 full seasons in Division One, they were again relegated in 1927. But that only paved the way for the club's greatest achievement as in 1930/31 they became the only side to win the double of FA Cup and promotion in the same season.

Relegation gathered the Baggies up one more in 1937/38 and Albion played just one full season in Division Two before 'proper' league games were once again suspended, due to the hostilities of war. Although football remained the staple diet of the sports fans throughout the dark days of 1939-45, it was only wartime competition, and could never replicate the atmosphere of Football League competition. Once normality returned, it took Albion just two seasons to get back to Division One, promotion secured at the end of the 1948/49 campaign. That began the longest run so far at the top of English football, as 24 full seasons would elapse before Albion would return to the Second Division. Albion would win the FA Cup on two further occasions, 1954 and 1968, and the League Cup before relegation loomed in 1972/73 under Don Howe. Johnny Giles replaced him to rejuvenate the club as player-manager, culminating in promotion at Oldham at the end of 1975/76, ten top-flight seasons following, including some extraordinary football. But Albion ended it potless and after a decade, 1985/86 became perhaps the grisliest season on record as the Baggies tumbled to relegation in a dreadful campaign.

Just when it looked like it couldn't get any worse, it did. Defeat to Woking in the FA Cup, the appointment of Bobby Gould, and relegation to the Third Division for the first time in Albion's history in 1990/91. We couldn't even make the play-offs at the first time of asking so Ossie Ardiles was charged with lightening the mood, something he achieved as the Throstles reached the old Wembley for the final time, defeating Port Vale in the play-off final of 1992/93, before Ardiles departed for Spurs. For the rest of the decade, Albion looked more likely to be relegated than get promoted but in 2001/02, a huge points deficit was overhauled, Wolves were overtaken, and Gary Megson's team were in the Premier League for the first time. And thus began the yo-yo years – relegation in 2002/03, promotion 12 months later, the 'Great Escape' of 2004/05, followed by the drop a year later. It took two years to get back this time, but the Throstles did it in style as champions under Tony Mowbray, also reaching the FA Cup semi-final. Relegation grasped Albion to its ample bosom once more before, in his first season as head coach, Roberto Di Matteo saw Albion through to yet another promotion from the Football League Championship to the Premier League.

CAPTAINS MARVEL

Towards the end of the 1968/69 season, Albion managed to get through three different captains in the space of just five days. On March 5th 1969, Albion travelled to Hillsborough to face Sheffield Wednesday and the job was in the capable hands of club captain for that season, Doug Fraser. Albion went down 1-0 in front of 18,960 spectators and unfortunately Fraser got himself injured and had to be replaced by John Kaye as the captain for the visit of Chelsea at The Hawthorns three days later on March 8th. Albion crashed once again, this time 3-0 to the men from Stamford Bridge, revenge after Albion had beaten them in the FA Cup in London a week before. The injury hoodoo once again struck Albion as skipper Kaye was also injured and was forced to miss the next three games, including the away visit to Roker Park, Sunderland, just two days later. This time, former captain Graham Williams assumed the mantle as Tony Brown's goal assured Albion of at least one win that week!! The attendance was a meagre 15,769 for a game that signalled the arrival of Len Cantello.

ON THE PASSING OF SIR BOBBY ROBSON, 2009

Football is an extraordinary game. Whenever it is at its most obnoxious, its ugliest, its most depressing, whenever it is wallowing in a periodic orgy of obscenity, when it is preoccupied with wealth, with off-the-field folly, it somehow pops up and gives us a reminder of why it is the people's game, the greatest game in the world, the game we loved as children, the game that possesses us as adults.

That antidote comes when we concentrate on the green rectangle, the altar around which we commune week after week, the gash of colour that illuminates workaday lives lived largely in monochrome, 22 coloured dots dancing around it, in myriad patterns, offering flashes of vision where we transcend where we are and we go to another place. Just as Brian Sewell can fall into rapture about a Michelangelo hung in the National Gallery, so too can we see the spark at the end of God's fingers in an electrifying piece of skill, impudence or trickery found at the feet of a footballer momentarily touched by magic.

What football generates is enthusiasm, wonder, excitement. We all feel it, but sometimes the spectacle of the game is lost beneath the spectacle it makes of itself. In those times, we need reminders of what makes the game special. Sadly, the death of Sir Bobby Robson was one of those reminders, because even amidst the sadness that surrounded his passing, it was memories of his enthusiasm for the game, the infectious smile, the pure joy that he got from football that beamed out from newspaper pages, TV tributes and website eulogies.

The passing of Sir Bobby on the eve of a new season was at once a personal tragedy for his family and friends, a perhaps merciful personal release from the foul ravages of cancer, a heartbreaking loss to a game crying out for the wisdom of its elders, and a timely reminder that football is a game that exists in hearts and souls, not in chequebooks and nightclubs.

Few, if any, footballing personalities have been so admired, respected, revered, and yes, genuinely loved by the footballing populace, as Sir Bobby. We saw that a couple of years ago when he received the BBC's Lifetime Achievement Award during the *Sports Personality of the Year* show. The standing ovation threatened to last all night long and Sir Bobby was visibly moved by the warmth of the tribute.

He could not have deserved the ovation, nor the award itself, more. Whether you agree with his views or not, be it back in the days when he was England manager, or more recently as a newspaper and occasional TV or radio pundit, you can't help but have the greatest affection for the man. For as Sir Alex Ferguson said as he presented him with that BBC award, there are few, if any, people who have such an unquenchable and contagious enthusiasm for the game of football, few who could talk about it all day long with such passion, such optimism, such love. He lived and breathed the game and in doing so, he became one of its immense characters, the kind who feed the game itself, give it its lifeblood. As football men go, Sir Bobby Robson is up there with the greatest of all, Saint Bill Shankly and Sir Matt Busby. There are no higher compliments, as Robson himself would recognise.

The bulk of Robson's renown was won in international football and, ultimately, it was for his career as England manager that people best remember him. And why not? It was a career that saw him take the nation to within a penalty kick of a World Cup final, far and away our greatest achievement since Geoff Hurst lashed that fourth goal into the roof of the Wembley net in 1966.

But before that, back in his days as a Throstle, Bobby Robson could play. Twenty England caps in an era where the national side played perhaps half the games it does today is a lasting legacy to the quality of his football as an inside-forward and then as a right-half, dropping back deeper in the side to a position where his vision and his passing could do yet more damage.

Robson came to The Hawthorns in March 1956 for the considerable sum of £25,000, leaving Fulham for the Black Country, having learned his craft at Craven Cottage by playing alongside another England legend, Johnny Haynes. He didn't come into a bad Albion team either, initially playing up front alongside Ronnie Allen and Derek Kevan before manager Vic Buckingham recognised that Robson's impeccable reading of the game would be better suited to a deeper lying role where the attacking play was laid out in front of him and he could pull the strings in the same style as the great Ray Barlow. He also came across another up-and-coming Albion player who was to have a big part in his career once he had hung up his boots, right-back Don Howe.

A first England cap came his way in November 1957, a friendly against the French, if such a thing exists. Robson played a full part in England's 4-0 win, scoring twice and placing himself at the forefront of the minds of the national selectors, crucial with a World Cup in Sweden in the offing the following summer. Playing at inside-right, he was replaced for the next three games by Bobby Charlton, still somewhat fragile after the horrors of the Munich air crash.

But by the time England manager Walter Winterbottom was formulating the team for the World Cup in tandem with the selection committee, Robson had played himself back into everyone's thoughts. He recaptured the number eight shirt for a friendly in Moscow, impressed in a 1-1 draw, and played in all three of the group games in Sweden, the opener being a 2-2 draw against the USSR, a game not without controversy, Robson having a goal ruled out: "The referee, Zsolt, was a Hungarian and that was at the time when they were being suppressed, threatened by the Russians, so there was controversy about his appointment. Whether that had anything to do with him disallowing a perfectly good goal, I don't know!" England drew 2-2 with the USSR, 0-0 with Brazil, then 2-2 with Austria, leading to a play-off which Robson sat out as the USSR sent England out of the tournament.

It took Robson two years to get back in the England picture, by which time he was playing as a half-back, in the midfield. He went on a summer tour and played in games against Spain and Hungary, which England lost comfortably, but clearly Robson had make his mark and he became a regular fixture in a side that also included players such as Jimmy Armfield, Bobby Charlton, his former Fulham colleague Johnny Haynes and England's greatest-ever goalscorer, Jimmy Greaves.

Over the next two-year period, Robson was fortunate enough to play in some incredible games for England, not least the famous 9-3 win over Scotland at Wembley in April 1961. Bobby opened the scoring, then Greaves helped himself to a hat-trick, Bobby Smith and Haynes weighing in with two each and Bryan Douglas completing the rout.

A second World Cup beckoned as Robson was in the party that headed out to prepare for the 1962 competition in Chile. England prepared by playing a friendly in Peru, as Robson recalled: "Bobby Moore went as cover for me. Walter Winterbottom rested me for that game, gave Bobby a run out to save me for the World Cup. We had a practice game and I fractured my ankle, got a crack in it, which was a three-week job, and Bobby Moore played instead of me. And that was Bobby in forever – 108 caps! We played Brazil in a knockout game and I was fit for that but not match fit, so Bobby stayed in. I was despondent about that, so upset, because I felt I'd been playing well."

That was Robson's England career finished, his final game turning out to be the May 9th 1962 game against the Swiss at Wembley. He'd finished with Albion too, for on his return to England, he left The Hawthorns to return to Fulham for £20,000, returning to London where, with the maximum wage ceiling's abolition in August 1961, Johnny Haynes had become the first

£100-a-week footballer. For Robson, an international and Albion captain, it was a chance to get something like the reward his talent deserved, because hitherto, he'd been supplementing his salary by working in the afternoons after training, selling steel tubes as a sideline. Never shy of a bit of graft, when he spoke of it 40 years later, you could still sense it was an affront to his professionalism that he couldn't dedicate himself solely to the game.

It was a grievous loss to the Throstles for though Albion hadn't quite got their hands on another trophy in his years, they were still good years as they regularly threatened a trip to Wembley, losing in the semi-final of the FA Cup in 1957, the sixth round a year later, while we were habitual visitors to the top half of the First Division table. Robson's drive, enthusiasm and culture were key elements of our play and he was missed.

It was inevitable that he should move into coaching after the game, Robson giving the credit for that shift to Walter Winterbottom, England's manager throughout his time with the national side, and a visionary as far as the technical side of the game went. Both he and Howe were bitten by the bug at his behest, Robson recalling, "Walter urged me and Don to go to Lilleshall to take up coaching under his guidance". As a consequence, the two were in the vanguard of the coaching revolution that started to bear fruit through the late 1960s and beyond.

After tough times in a brief spell at Fulham, Robson settled in at Ipswich Town. There too he had his share of battles with senior pros early on, but for all the avuncular nature of the man, there was a steely streak there too and he fought it out before going on to build a glorious football team in Suffolk, although the rotten so-and-so didn't need to go and beat the Albion in the 1978 FA Cup semi, did he?

Ipswich were a perfect exposition of Robson's footballing philosophies, especially once the likes of Muhren and Thijssen had been added to players such as Talbot and Wark. They were intelligent, tactically sophisticated and hard as nails when they needed to be. It's a great shame that they never quite took the First Division title they should have, most notably missing out in 1981 when Villa pipped them to it, Ipswich burdened by a heavy fixture load that brought its consolation in the shape of the Uefa Cup at the end of that campaign.

Success in Europe made him the natural successor to Ron Greenwood after he stepped down as England boss in 1982, Robson embarking on the typical rollercoaster ride that each England manager endures, cast as hero and villain, often on the same day.

Ultimately, by reaching the semi-finals of Italia 1990, Robson became second only to Alf Ramsey in terms of success with the national side. Interviewing him several years ago for a book on the history of the England side, was a particular privilege. One thing he said that day remains one of the most memorable quotes anyone has ever served up to me.

"I was lucky enough to play with people like Tom Finney, Duncan Edwards, Bobby Charlton, Jimmy Greaves – great, great footballers who loved playing for England. Then over the years, the players I selected, guys like Gary Lineker, Peter Beardsley, Bryan Robson, Paul Gascoigne, Ray Wilkins, Gary Mabbutt, they all felt the same way we did. There is a great passion about the English players and in all the eight years I was in charge, I never met a player who wasn't just absolutely captivated and thrilled by their selection. It isn't easy to play for England in that spotlight, but they all want that chance. Some are nervous about it, and it takes some four or five internationals before they feel comfortable, before they can put on that white shirt, stand on the pitch at Wembley, and be themselves. Some, like Gascoigne, just take to it. He played his first game as though he'd played 50 times, but others, you know they've got the talent and the character, but the occasion gets to them. But I never found a player who wasn't captivated by it, and that's as it should be."

That was how it was for Robson, enthusiast to the last, through the club coaching career that followed England, success at PSV Eindhoven, Porto, Barcelona and Newcastle United, and through the bouts of cancer that did their best to beat him into submission. Nobody can escape the ravages of time and Robson was no exception, but in what fashion did he rage glorious against the dying of the light! Knowing that finally, there would be no remission, no escape from the reaper, Sir Bobby did not meekly accept his fate.

Instead, he used his name and his reputation to the full, throwing it all behind the Sir Bobby Robson Foundation, a charity that focuses on the early detection and treatment of cancer and the clinical trials of new drugs that will eventually beat it. It has already raised millions, but there is much work still to be done – you can help by donating at http://www. justgiving.com/thesirbobbyrobsonfoundation/

What remains to be said? Sir Bobby taught us lessons on how to play the game. More important, he taught us how to cherish it, how to love it, nurture it, breathe with it, bleed for it. The game is desperately, desperately impoverished with his passing. But if we remember the things he stood for, for football, for tradition, history, for the escape the game brings, the feeling it engenders, the smiles it offers, the invisible umbilical cord it stretches across generations, father to son to son to son, then we will honour his memory the way he would want. Black armbands and minute's silences are right and proper. But loving the game, protecting it, relishing it, that is the living legacy he leaves behind. What better life's work than that?

Rest easy Sir Bobby.